how to BREW Honey WINE

KARL STÜCKLER

Schiffer Publishing Ltd
4880 Lower Valley Road • Atglen, PA 19310

Other Schiffer Books on Related Subjects:

The Perfect Sausage: Making and Preparing Homemade Sausage,
Karsten "Ted" Aschenbrandt, hard cover, 120pp. ISBN: 978-0-7643-4302-5. $19.99
The Big Smoker Book,
Karsten "Ted" Aschenbrandt and Rudolf Jaeger. ISBN: 978-0-7643-4328-5, hard cover, 152pp. $34.99
Distilling Fruit Brandy.
Josef Pischl. ISBN: 978-0-7643-3926-4, hard cover, 176pp. $34.99

Photo credits: All images were provided by the author.

Originally published as *Met, Honigwein-Bereitung leicht gemacht!*
by Leopold Stocker Verlag, Graz - Stuttgart, 2011.
Translated by Omicron Language Solutions, LLC

Library of Congress Control Number: 2013938364

Type set in ITC Symbol

ISBN: 978-0-7643-4457-2
Printed in China

Published by Schiffer Publishing, Ltd.
4880 Lower Valley Road
Atglen, PA 19310
Phone: (610) 593-1777; Fax: (610) 593-2002
E-mail: Info@schifferbooks.com

In Europe, Schiffer books are distributed by
Bushwood Books
6 Marksbury Ave.
Kew Gardens
Surrey TW9 4JF England
Phone: 44 (0) 20 8392 8585; Fax: 44 (0) 20 8392 9876
E-mail: info@bushwoodbooks.co.uk
Website: www.bushwoodbooks.co.uk

Contents

Preface

During my work, both teaching and consulting at the Beekeepers' School in Warth-Aichhof (Lower Austria), I realized several years ago that there is little useful literature available about mead. In 1995, Leopold Stocker Verlag published my book *Mead*, which represents to date a standard reference work on brewing mead. Now, it is time to revise this book. Both recent insights and the experience from more than twenty years of brewing mead have helped create this completely new book.

Mead is both brewed by amateur wine makers for their own consumption and made in larger quantities by beekeepers, who have built a separate line of business from mead production. This book should offer valuable assistance to both.

The first part of the book includes, in the chapter "The science of mead for small producers," page 21, the most important work steps; by following these steps, with a little effort and a small investment, it is possible to produce a drinkable mead. The chapter "The broader science of mead," page 33, includes more in-depth information about fermentation, fining (purification), stabilization, and bottling. Analytical values and methods for testing, mead faults and diseases, as well as legal requirements, complete the subject.

The mead brewer's goal must be to make a wholesome, high quality and, above all, stable honey wine in attractive packaging. Only when you have mastered the art of honey wine making, bringing together alcohol, residual sugar and acidity into a harmonious balance—through fault-free fermentation—will it be possible to convince consumers to try this high-quality product.

This book will help you get a few steps closer to that goal. I wish you good success.

Ritterburg Lockenhaus
Asgard
Met
Ritterburg Lockenhaus
A-7442 Lockenhaus
Tel. +43 2616 2394, Fax DW -80
www.ritterburg.at
0,5l
L 100/07/04 - Kühl lagern!
12%vol

Introduction

The history of honey wine

Traditions with mead in Austria, Germany and Switzerland

What influences the flavor of honey wine

Mead is becoming ever more important for modern beekeeping. The demand for high quality honey wines is rising, while mead also offers more and more beekeepers a means to expand their product range. At the same time, retail prices for blossom honey (rapeseed, locust and sunflower honey) are often low, which inclines the beekeeper to attempt to create a higher-priced product from his honey.

Beekeepers are increasingly brewing mead as a separate business.

Offering good quality mead will increase the demand, and open a lucrative market niche for beekeepers.

Formerly, mead was brewed following old recipes; today, the aim is not to rigidly follow a formula, but rather – adapted to the product – be able to flexibly and economically produce a stable/sound honey wine corresponding to what consumers want. Today, due to both technical innovations in wine making and greater knowledge in the field of microbiology, there are better options for brewing mead.

You don't require recipes, but rather adequate expertise in fermentation techniques and enology, the science of wine making, as well as competence in marketing. Today, you can create more types of flavor with mead, than with any other drink.

The key factors crucial for the taste and structure of honey wine:

- Type of honey
- Flavoring
- Water or fruit juice base
- Fermentation conditions
- Final alcohol content
- Residual sugar content

These are only the most important factors. Of course, then come storage conditions, selecting the yeast, bottling procedures, etc. This all adds up to all the possible ways to brew, so that no mead will be like any other. To be able to offer your own customers as consistent a taste as possible, it is important to keep regular records. Whatever type of mead the producer decides to brew, it is important that only pure flavored, faultless mead goes on the market. Inferior products will discourage consumers, and they will lose interest in buying mead again.

Only high quality mead should reach the market.

You can make mead with a very large variety of flavors, as mentioned above. With all this diversity, we recognize three completely different types of mead:

Classic honey wine (classic mead)

This is characterized by its delicate touch of honey. The residual sugar content is usually between 80 to 140 grams per liter. Only water and honey are used in brewing. It resembles mild and sweet grape wines, with its fine notes of honey and raisins. The target customers are sweet wine drinkers, who have discovered mead as a secret.

Dry-aged honey wine

In this mead, the honey's sugar content has been completely converted to alcohol – and it is not sweetened after fermentation. This wine does not have the sweet honey character. Chestnut and lime tree honey give a tart character; rapeseed honey will produce, in fully fermented mead, a taste with a real edge to it. Since most mead consumers have a more or less sweet product in mind, this group of honey wines has fewer fans. But there are excellent dry-aged honey wines, which are a real pleasure for the connoisseur.

Honey wine mixed with spices and fruit juices

Dragon's blood, Odin's blood, Viking blood, or the devil's blood: these are just a few of the names for mead with cherry juice. Some spices were also added to this drink. The origin of these recipes comes from Norse mythology, when a pair of dwarves, Fjalar and Galar, killed the giant Kvasir and mixed his blood with honey to make mead. Odin stole and drank this mead, which gave him wings, so he could fly into the intermediate world to Asgard. During the Middle Ages, friends would drink such honey wines together.

Mead can be brewed with many different types of flavors.

Apple juice can also be a welcome addition. Such added ingredients not only affect the mead's final taste, but such honey wines ferment better due to the added, freshly pressed juices.

You can also brew and serve pure herbal and spiced meads. There are all sorts of traditional recipes in circulation. There should be no limit to the imagination when adding flavorings. For these meads, the main customer is a health-conscious consumer who likes the combination of honey with the positive effect of herbs.

To achieve good quality, it is necessary to acquire an in-depth knowledge of fermenting technique and enology.

This book is intended to provide a detailed basic knowledge for the interested mead brewer, and at the same time give them an incentive to attempt brewing their own mead.

The history of honey wine

The history of honey wine is closely related to the history of honey, which goes back to the Stone Age. Cave drawings, like those in the Cueva de la Araña near Valencia in Spain, which are estimated to be 16,000 years old, provide vivid information on this.

Historically, mead is the oldest alcoholic beverage.

For all civilized people, honey always represented something choice, and with it came mead. It may have been merely by accident that honey was diluted with water, began to ferment, and produced an intoxicating drink.

In the harems of the Arabs, a mixture of mead and coconut milk, combined with fish, was thought to increase potency.

Indians call their mead "medhu," an especially treasured drink which is only served to guests of honor.

Mead is especially associated with the Romans and ancient Germans, and has not lost its image as a drink for strength, courage and health, even to this day.

Mead has this reputation thanks to the combination of alcohol with simple sugars (fructose and glucose from the honey). The alcohol lessens inhibitions, while sugar provides the necessary power.

The Gauls and Germans did not ferment their mead with just water, but also mixed it with barley and hops juice. The name "mead" for "honey wine" probably refers back to the Indo-European "medhu." Thus, honey and honey wine were already known by the Germans, Celts, and Slavs, in their aboriginal homeland.

One of the oldest mead recipes is found in *The Book of Good Food* from 1350.

One of the oldest surviving mead recipes is to be found in the Munich University library; it was composed in 1350 in Würzburg. The recipe is part of the cookbook *The Book of Good Food*. See the translated recipe below.

"The Honey Water," (woodcut from the Hortus Sanitatis, *Strasbourg, 1500)*

"Who wants to make good mead, warms clean water as much that you can still hold your hand in it. Take two measures of water and a measure of honey. Stir with a rod and let the whole sit for a while. Then strain it through a clean cloth or a fine sieve into a clean barrel. Boil it for as long as it takes to walk along a field there and back, and remove the foam with a perforated shell. The foam will stay in the shell, but not the liquid. Then, pour the mead into a clean barrel and cover it, so the steam can't escape, until you can hold your hand in it. Take a measuring cup and fill it half full of hops and a handful of sage, and boil at the same time with the mead, for a half-mile. Add this to the mead; take a half nut of fresh living yeast and add this also, mix it in thoroughly, so that it ferments. Cover it, so that the steam can escape, for a day and a night. Then filter the mead through a clean cloth or through a fine sieve. Pour it into a clean barrel and leave it three days and three nights to ferment, and rack it every night, then leave it again to rest, and protect it from intrusion by yeast, and let it set for eight days, so that it settles/clarifies, and rack it every night. Then pour it into a hardened, sealed barrel and let it stand for fully eight days and drink it within the next six or eight weeks. That is when it is best."

The length of a field: since there were no watches, the length of time it took to walk the distance of a field length was used.

½ mile: again a time period; how long you needed to walk this distance by foot.

½ nut: a quantity indicating as much as fits in half a nutshell.

Mead is a drink with a centuries-old tradition.

An important group of gingerbread bakers emerged around 1000 AD, in such places as Nuremberg, Straubing, Brunswick, and so forth, where mead was also brewed. They had their own authority to oversee the baking and quality of the gingerbread, as well as of the honey wine.

In *Meyer's Encyclopedia* of 1890 – more than 100 years ago – we find the following under "mead" (honey wine):

"Alcoholic liquor, which is prepared from honey, water and spices; about 17 percent alcohol; includes sugar, mannitol, organic acids etc. and is drunk especially in England, the east Flemish countries and some honey-rich regions of Germany, although no longer as generally as before. Mead is comparable to grape wine but it can be toxic if the honey was made from poisonous plants. To prepare mead, dissolve honey in water, boil it, skim off the foam, add hops; other possible ingredients are fruit juice, cardamom, galangal root, coriander and nutmeg; and boil once again. The liquid is then put into a barrel, after cooling, yeast is added, and after fermentation is completed, the wine is poured into another bunged barrel, in which the mead will be kept for several months, after which it is bottled. After long aging, good mead is similar to Madeira. Mead was already

known to the Greeks and Romans, and, according to Pytheas, it was the usual drink of the Nordic population in the 4th century BC. In the 8th century AD, mead was the national drink in the Baltic countries, and is still drunk there today. In North Asia, South Africa, Ethiopia, and on Madagascar, honey was also used for preparing an intoxicating beverage."

Traditions and mead in Austria, Germany and Switzerland

Since year one, mead has been a prized stimulating drink and therefore has an important place in traditions. We have known the "mead boilers" since the Middle Ages. In the following centuries, up to the 20th, mead was an important drink at festive events, where it was primarily consumed by women.

Holidays gave a reason for drinking mead socially, such as during the pre-Easter "Confession days," Holy Week, Palm Sunday, at the annual parish fair on Corpus Christi, and the solstices, Christmas and at harvest time. Mead was also an integral part of any religious pilgrimage and wedding. In England, during earlier times, a bride would drink mead to increase her fertility for one month after her wedding. This custom has not been preserved over time, but we all know the expression "honeymoon."

Mead was formerly brewed by the Lebkuchen (gingerbread) bakers.

Many houses brewed their own mead, but generally it was produced commercially by the gingerbread bakers. There were times when, even in Bavaria, more mead was drunk than beer. The guild system in Bavaria only allowed the gingerbread bakers to brew and serve mead.

Josef Leuchtmüller, a Linz (Austria) gingerbread baker, wrote in his *Recipe book of 1699*:

"Take note: mead brewing takes a lot of care, but the gain is always great and can often compete with what we get from making gingerbread."

To store or transport the mead, people used "Metpitschen" [Austrian lialect for mead pitchers or jugs]. If a place had no gingerbread baker of :s own, then mead grocers would bring the mead and set up a market tall or a separate mead hut. Taverns and pastry shops also served mead.

Mead was usually drunk from glasses, but the use of mead buns or rolls s also reported (E. Burgstaller, Met im oberösterreichischen Brauchtum "Mead in Upper Austrian Traditions"], 1956). In the Inn river region, people ook smooth double rolls—not Kaiser rolls—hollowed them out with their ingers, poured the mead they had bought into the hollow, and closed it igain with the piece of roll. Then they carried this home. If the whole roll vas soaked through with mead, you just ate the bread. Usually, however, nead was enjoyed along with gingerbread and donuts.

Mead is a deeply rooted part of Alpine traditions.

At the solstice and grain reaping time, people made mead soup in many)laces in Upper Austria. Sweetened pieces of white bread or gingerbread vith hot mead poured over them went with the mead soup. At harvest time,)eople ate this mead soup in the belief that mead had a preventive effect igainst the dreaded backaches they suffered during reaping.

They also made the prized "Mete" or "Mölse" from mead with poppy ;eeds mixed in. This they poured over Krapfen, and gave them to young :hildren to suck, so that they would go to sleep.

In Pflaurenz, near St. Lorenzen, in Tyrol, people were known to make 'Metar" from honey, water and herbed mead, in the period around 1860. Their bee colony was killed by sulfur fumes (on the dung-heap or in a pit) ind the honeycombs were cut out, slowly brought to a boil in water and :ooled. The honey and water were then separated, and the remaining ioney passed through a fine sieve. Into the middle of the 19th century, 'Traunsteiner beer," a mixture of beer and mead, was served in taverns.

From: Maier-Bruck, Franz, *Vom Essen auf dem Lande* [*Countryside Eating*]. Publisher Kremayr & Scheriau, Vienna 1981.)

Influences on flavor

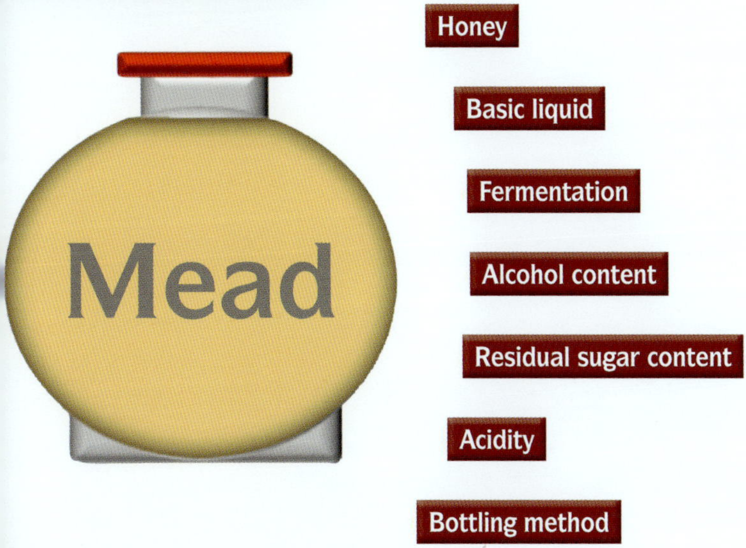

What influences the flavor of honey wine

Brewing mead is basically very simple. There are no "trade secrets," just different ways to get to the goal. The basic prerequisites for fault-free results are noted below:

Honey

Each type of honey creates a different flavor—mixed flower honey is generally used. Single-variety honey wines, such as linden (lime tree) honey mead, are available. In this sense, any kind of honey is suitable for brewing mead.

"Classic" honey wine is made of only honey and water.

Basic liquid

Water, fruit juice, or a fruit juice and water mixture are used for the basic liquid. The higher the proportion of fruit juice, the more the fruit character affects the honey wine. Cherry or apple juices are good choices. Classic honey wine is made only with water.

Fermentation

If there is any secret to making mead, it is in the process of fermentation and managing fermentation. How do you succeed in fermenting the honey you are using, to prevent faulty fermentation or a "stuck fermentation"? Is it best to follow the turn-of-the-century recipes, or trust the science of modern fermentation techniques?

Flavorings

Flavorings or spices are often used to cover up unpleasant flavors in the existing honey wine. In general, spices should be used sparingly, unless you intend to make a strongly spiced mead. Put no limits on your imagination in choosing spices: the consumer's nose and palate are what decide if a creation is successful.

Alcohol content

Alcohol content, acidity, and residual sugar content must be kept in a harmonious balance.

The higher the alcohol content, the more long-lived the product will be. Excessive alcohol content has an unfavorable effect on the palate: the mead will have a burning taste and will develop a mild alcoholic dominance. Honey wine with too little alcohol will be flat and short-lived on the palate. Due to the lower alcohol content, the residual sugar comes to the fore and the sweetness dominates.

Residual sugar

Residual sugar levels are generally between 80 and 140 grams per liter when alcohol levels are around 12% to 13% by volume, or ABV. Even honey wines that seem dry on the palate still have values between 10 and 20 grams per liter, due to unfermentable complex sugars. Yet such honey wines appear to be fully fermented to your senses, because the mineral content of the honey cushions the residual sugar.

The higher the alcohol content, the higher the residual sugar content can be, and the reverse is equally true.

Acidity

Neither honey nor water provides appropriate acidic body. If the acidity is not improved, a honey wine will appear flabby, dull and lifeless.

Apart from the sensory effect, it is also necessary to add acidity before fermentation, for microbiological preservation.

Bottling stable wine

What is the use of brewing the best honey wine if it starts to ferment in the bottle, if there are microbiological changes, or if proteins or other contents flocculate during longer bottle aging?

The science of mead for small producers

The easiest way to your own mead

This chapter is intended for small producers, who want to brew small amounts up to 52 quarts (50 liters) for their personal consumption. They generally do not have fining (purification) agents and filtration systems available to them, so that the product is usually slightly cloudy. This is not necessarily detrimental to the mead's quality, but you can expect that the lees will fall to the bottom during longer aging, which can detract from its appearance. Such honey wines are usually not bottled, but consumed directly from the barrel on festive occasions. Carboys or small plastic drums make good vessels. If you want a clear drink, there are small filter systems available, which are also used for filtering during distillation.

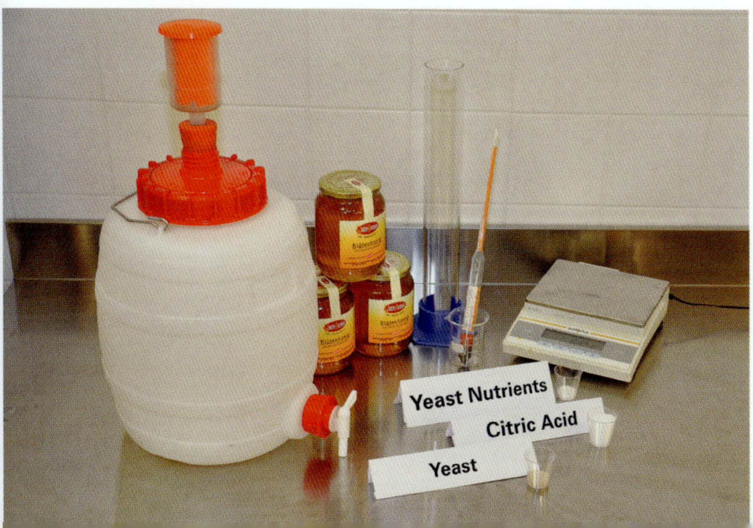

Basic equipment for making mead

Mead - a short guide

WHAT	WHY
Obtain 3 kg of the honey of your choice; it's best to get it from your local beekeeper.	You will get the best-quality honey from your beekeeper.
Warm the honey to 104° F (40° C) over boiling water.	The honey will liquify, but retain valuable ingredients.
Mix the honey with 7 l warm water.	With complete fermentation of the sugar, these proportions yield an alcohol content of approximately 13% to 14% ABV.
Let the honey-water mixture cool to 68°F (20° C). This mixture yields approximately 9 liters of mead. 1 kg of honey has a volume of 0.7 liter.	68° F (20°C) is the ideal temperature for stirring in the pure cultured yeast.
Mix in 20 g of citric acid.	This increases the acidity, making the starter more resistant to bacterial infections, and the added acidity gives the finished mead a fresher taste.
Now add 4 g of a combination of yeast nutrients (containing all the important ingredients for yeast nutrition, such as N, P and vitamins).	You will get a clean fermentation if the yeast has optimal nutrition.
Add 6.4 g yeast nutrient	Yeast nutrition and choice of yeast are the decisive points in preparing mead. We need a vigorously fermenting yeast with a high alcohol yield.
Close the container with a fermentation tube, that you previously filled with water.	Fermentation gases can escape, but the oxygen from air cannot enter.
Keep away from sunlight and pay attention to maintaining a constant fermentation temperature of about 64.4°F (18° C).	Too high a fermentation temperature leads to loss of alcohol and aroma, too low leads to a stuck fermentation.

WHAT	WHY
After two to three weeks, the intensity of fermentation subsides; you can stir carefully with a cooking spoon.	This stimulates the yeast, increasing the fermenting intensity, so the remaining sugar can ferment completely.
When fermentation finally stops (after 2 more weeks), the mead must be separated from the settled yeast. This is done most easily by carefully emptying it into a new vessel, leaving the lees behind – racking.	If the mead stays on the yeast, this inevitably leads the mead to serious diseases, such as “mousiness,” or a sulfur off-taste and smell.
If fermentation has gone optimally, the mead will have around 13% ABV and taste somewhat sweet on the palate.	If the mead, after fermentation, doesn't seem sweet enough, you can add more honey to create the optimal residual sugar content.
By adding more honey, you obtain the optimal residual sugar content. For this, warm the honey of your choice, dissolve it in a small amount of mead, and stir it in carefully.	If, after you added honey, the mead starts to ferment again, this is not a drawback. The alcohol content will increase and decrease the adjusted residual sugar. But it will be necessary to rack the mead again off the resulting yeast.
The amount of added honey can be up to 700 g, depending on taste; the more, the sweeter your mead will be.	It is best to add the honey to the mead starting solution carefully, while tasting constantly, so you maintain the optimum residual sugar content.
Due to fermentation and adding more honey, the mead will still be cloudy. But there is nothing in the way of enjoying it. If the mead seems too limp or insipid, adding up to a maximum 20 g citric acid will compensate.	The mead is ready, but still cloudy, but the lees ingredients (yeast) will settle more during longer aging and the mead will become clearer. Another racking will improve clarity.

1
Blütenhonig
2
3
4
5
6
7
8
9
10
11
ZITRONENSÄURE
Blütenhonig
12

Mead – a description

Selecting the honey

There are so many different kinds of honey, and all this diversity is reflected in the flavor of the mead.

Basically, any type of honey is suitable, like everywhere else in life it is ultimately a matter of taste. But there are some varieties with distinctive flavors that strongly influence the mead. A mixture of rapeseed and locust honey produces mead with a subtle, fruity note, which does not appear coarse and is widely acceptable to consumers. Sunflower and forest honeys give a broad body, sometimes heavy, and are strong on the palate.

If you intend to make spiced mead or mead to mix with fruit juices, the choice of honey plays less of a role – the spices and the juice will be the dominant flavor components.

Figure 1: *Heat 3 kg of honey over hot water to 104° F (40° C).*

Figure 2: *Pour 1 l hot water into the fermentation vessel.*

Figure 3: *Dissolve the heated honey in the hot water.*

Figure 4: *Add 6 liters cold water and mix together the vessel contents.*

Figure 5: *The starter solution now has a sugar content of about 25°Brix.*

Figure 6: *Dissolve 20 g citric acid and 4 g of yeast nutrients in a small amount of mead, and stir into the starter.*

Figure 7: *Add 3 g previously rehydrated, dry, pure culture yeast.*

Figure 8: *Seal the fermentation tank with a fermentation tube. The fermentation period is about 2-3 weeks at 64.4° F (18° C). Normally, this will produce 13-14% ABV.*

Figure 9: *After fermentation ends, the fermented mead is racked off the lees.*

Figure 10: *A view of the lees at the bottom of the barrel*

Figure 11: *Depending on your preference, the taste of the mead can be rounded out with up to 700 g of honey and up to 20 g of citric acid. Due to the high alcohol content, the mead should not start fermenting again.*

Figure 12: *The mead is now ready, but cloudy. After longer aging in completely filled containers, you will see the lees fall to the bottom. If you want a clear mead, it must be fined and filtered. More on this in later chapters.*

Mead starter solution

Alcohol is made from fermenting the sugar in the honey. The higher the sugar content of the honey-water/fruit juice mixture, the higher the alcohol content, but also the longer the fermentation period.

It isn't necessary to "boil" the mead starter solution.

> To avoid having to sweeten the fermented mead, we recommend proportions of 2 liters of water with 1 kg honey.

However, this will mean a significantly longer fermentation, due to the high sugar concentration.

When you use a vigorously fermenting yeast, you can obtain about 14% ABV, with a balanced residual sugar content after fermentation.

In the old recipes, the mead starter is boiled to deactivate any wild yeasts. The resulting mead is more viscous, proteins are completely eliminated before fermentation and the color darkened by caramelization.

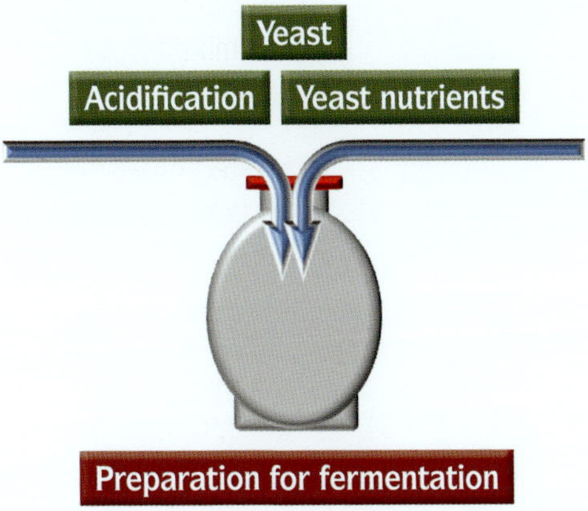

Preparing for fermentation

To achieve a clean, pure fermentation, both rapid start fermentation and brisk fermentation are absolutely necessary. To prepare for fermenting your mead, you need 25 g per 100 liters of vigorously fermenting yeast, you then should add enough yeast nutrients 40 g/100 liters.
The water-honey mixture does not contain natural acids and thus:

Conscientious preparation is the basic requirement for an optimal fermentation process.

1. it can be limp and flabby on the palate
2. it has a higher pH value,

which are optimal conditions for proliferation of undesired microorganisms such as acetic, lactic and butyric acid bacteria. It is necessary to add liquid lactic acid 240 ml/100 liters, or 200 g/100 l of citric acid.

Fermentation

- The ideal fermentation temperature is between 62.6 and 68°F (17 and 20° C).
- Fermentation should start within 24 hours.
- Seal the barrel with a stopper.
- The fermentation process must be monitored continuously (tasting, CO_2 development, temperature).

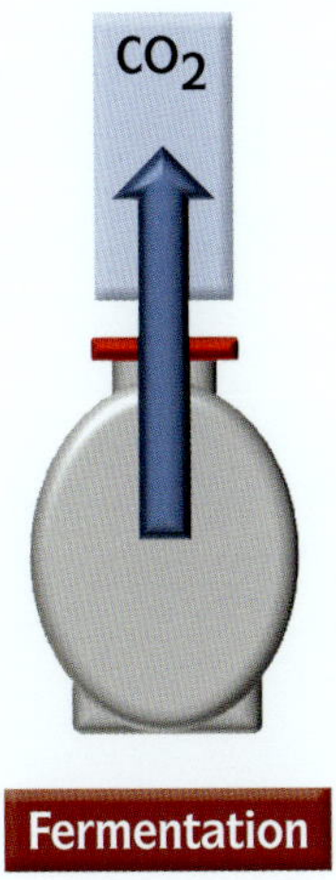

Racking after primary fermentation

In contrast to other drinks, when brewing mead you must rack it off the resulting lees as soon as fermentation is coming to an end the first time. Failure to do so creates a serious risk that the drink will be spoiled by bacterial infections.

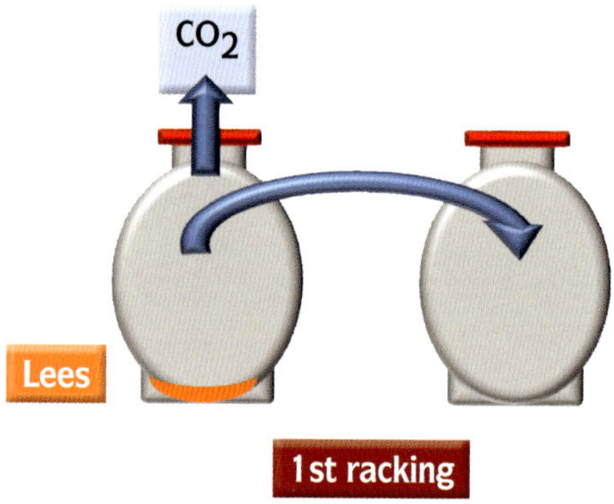

Racking after fermentation is complete

After the stormy primary fermentation and first separation of the honey wine from the settled yeast (also known as "decanting" or "racking" off the yeast sediment), the next is a secondary fermentation phase, which can last for weeks, when only small amounts of carbon dioxide are generated. The fermentation stopper (fermentation tube) "jumps" only occasionally. When this stops completely, the mead is ready to rack again. When you taste it, if you suspect there is something adversely affecting the taste, you should rack the mead off the dregs earlier.

After fermentation is complete, the mead is racked off the yeast.

Depending on the proportion of honey to water, the pure culture yeast used and fermentation conditions, more or less residual sugar will be left over from fermentation. In general, mead is a crude product after fermentation, which can be refined by adding spices or more honey.

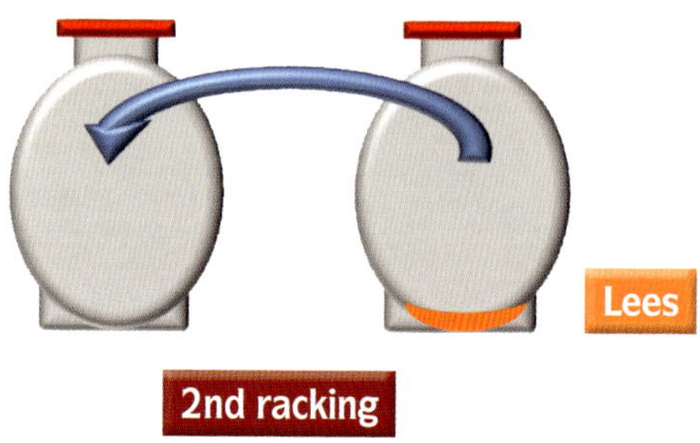

Adjusting residual sugar

If you find the remaining residual sugar out of balance and too low, you can compensate by adding more honey (flavorful blossom honeys are best). Since the risk of re-fermentation in the bottle is primarily due to an alcohol content that is too low, such meads should be bottled hot (149°F or 65°C). This temperature kills yeast cells and prevents re-fermentation.

Adjusting residual sugar

Filtration

For small amounts, liquor filters are suitable. Using a hand pump, which creates excess pressure, the mead is pressed through cellulose layers, which trap the lees. Depending on the type of filter used, you get a coarser or finer filtration.

Fining makes filtration easier.

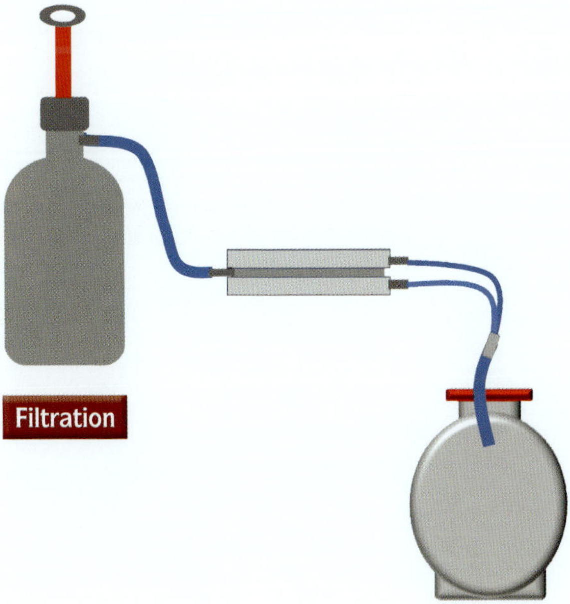

Filtration

Adding wine sulfur

To prevent oxidation and unwanted growth of negative micro-organisms, and to bind with fermentation by-products, 1.2 g per 10 liters of wine sulfur (potassium pyrosulphite, usually called potassium metabisulfite) should be added after fermentation has ended (exact measurement is necessary).

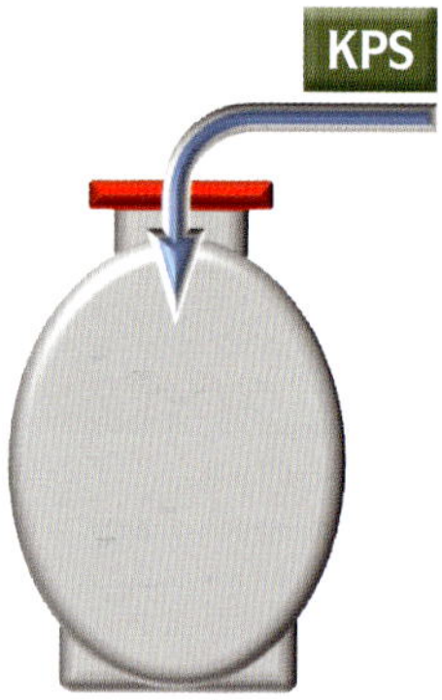

Adding wine sulfur

Spices

Spices should complement in a balanced way, not dominate.

Old recipes provide vivid information about this aspect of mead brewing. There is no limit to the ingenuity you can use combining spices.

Whether you add them directly or hang them in the mead in linen bags, if you add them before or after fermentation or during aging, is all up to the brewer.

The basic principle to use is: If you add any spices, they should complement in a balanced way, and not dominate!

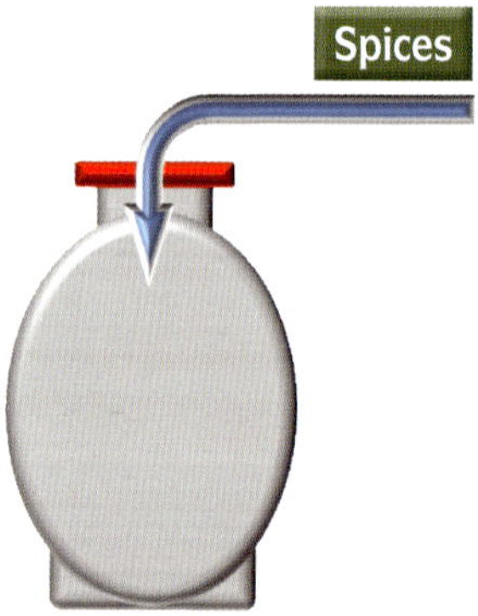

Adding flavorings

Aging and bottling

Long-term aging can increase the balance of a mead with high alcohol and residual sugar content. Using healthy, oak barrels can create an additional aging effect, such as enhanced color. The ideal storage temperature is between 50 and 59° F (10 and 15° C).

The alcohol and the residual sugar contents of the honey wine are decisive factors when choosing your bottling method.

GOAL: To bottle the mead so that there can be no re-fermentation!

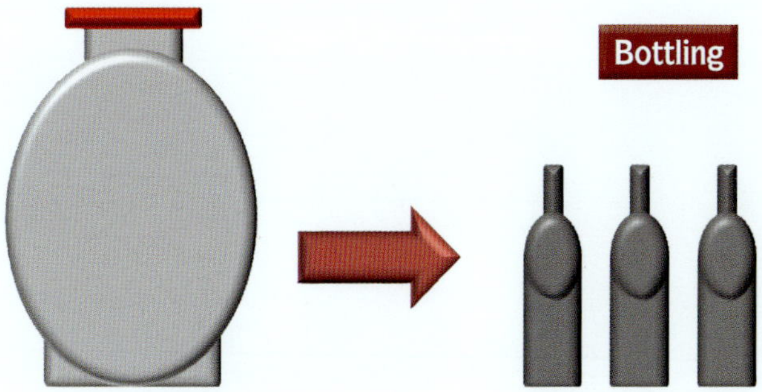

MET
AUS

The Broader Science of Mead

General description of method

METHODS FOR BREWING MEAD	
Long fermentation phase	**Short fermentation phase**
Closer proportions of honey to water/fruit juice	Broader proportions of honey to water/fruit juice
(higher sugar content) in the starter solution	(lower sugar content) in the starter solution
with high sugar levels ■ slower start of fermentation ■ long fermentation time ■ lower alcohol content ■ higher residual sugar content	**with lower sugar content** ■ more rapid start of fermentation ■ short fermentation time ■ higher alcohol content ■ full fermentation
	BUT: later adjustment of residual sugar level necessary

Long fermentation

This is the traditional method of making mead. To begin, the honey-water and fruit juice mixture has such a high sugar concentration that it is impossible for the yeast to convert it completely into alcohol. The yeast can generally only create an ABV up to about 14%. In exceptional cases, you can get a higher alcohol content. The yeast dies in its own product, the alcohol. If you look at old recipes, the sugar level is often so high that about 18 to 20% ABV could develop theoretically. But this high level of sugar concentration inhibits the yeast in the beginning phase of fermentation as well as during fermentation, so an alcohol level of about 10% ABV is usually yielded, with an extremely high residual sugar content.

The broader science of mead

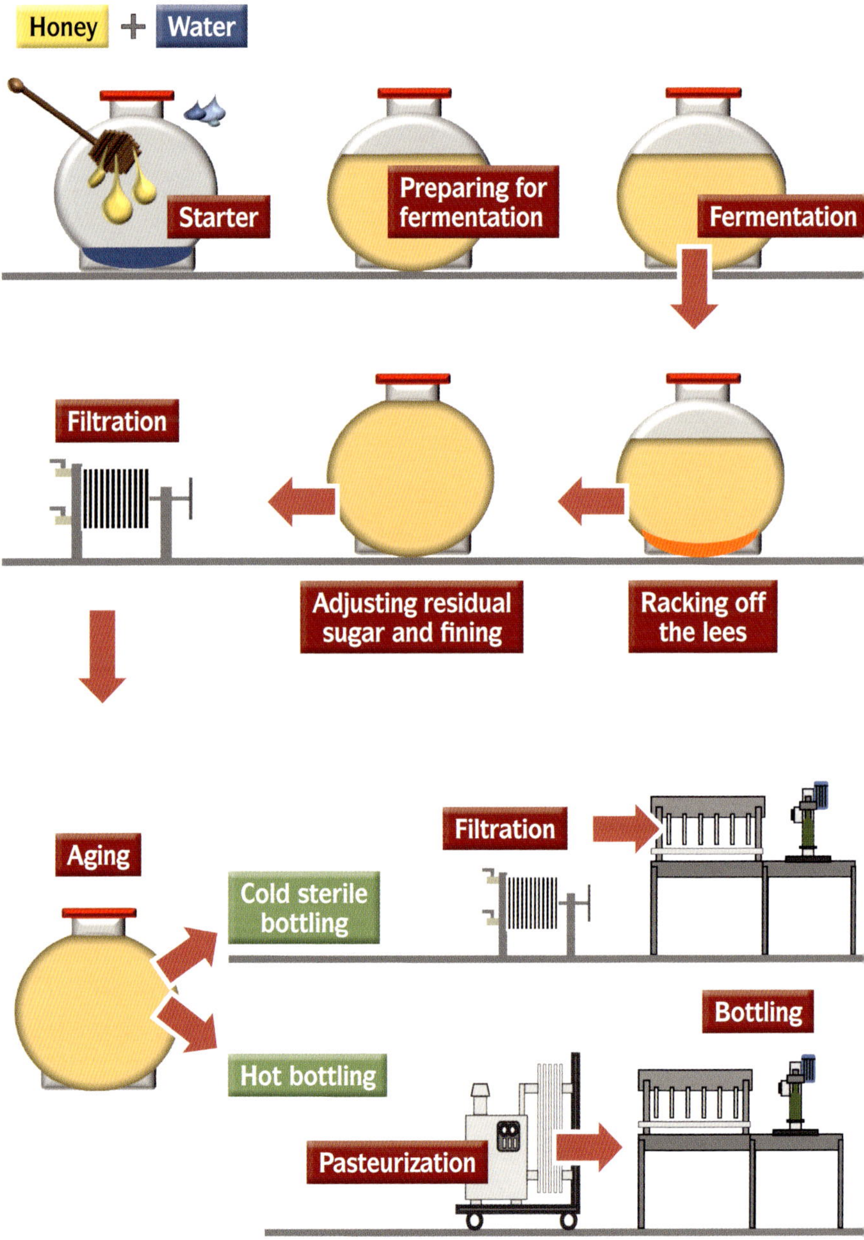

The fermentation period takes a half year and longer. The residual sugar level can barely be controlled, so that it is mostly a product of chance, depending upon the yeast used.

High sugar concentration in the starter solution causes a long fermentation time.

Along with the noted disadvantages, we should not forget the benefits:

- Such honey wine does not have to be sweetened – it is balanced and well-rounded.
- Potential re-fermentation in the bottle is highly unlikely, and germ-free bottle filling is sufficient.

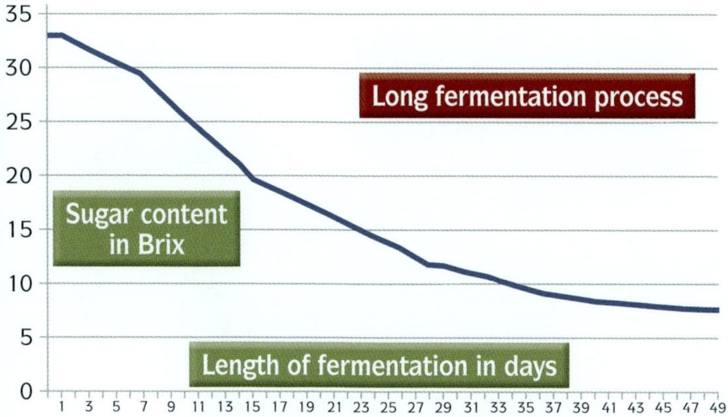

Short fermentation

The sugar concentration of the water-honey mixture is adjusted so that the yeast can ferment completely, leaving hardly any residual sugar after fermentation. Exact adjustment of the residual sugar level is only done shortly before bottling, after preliminary tests.

This method offers many advantages:

- Rapid fermentation: reduces the risk of faulty fermentation or bacterial infection
- You can ensure a constant residual sugar content from one batch of mead to the next.
- You can produce various types of mead with differing residual sugar levels (medium sweet/mild, sweet, etc.) from one basic mead.

There are also risks to consider:

- If the alcohol content is too low after the basic mead is fermented (under 13% ABV), there is a risk of renewed fermentation after the residual sugar is adjusted.
- A small producer should generally bottle such honey wines "warm" (pasteurization) – a larger enterprise will choose "cold sterile bottling" (see chapter "Bottling," page 93.).

With a sugar content of 26° Brix (= 110 °Oe), fermentation is complete after about 30 days.

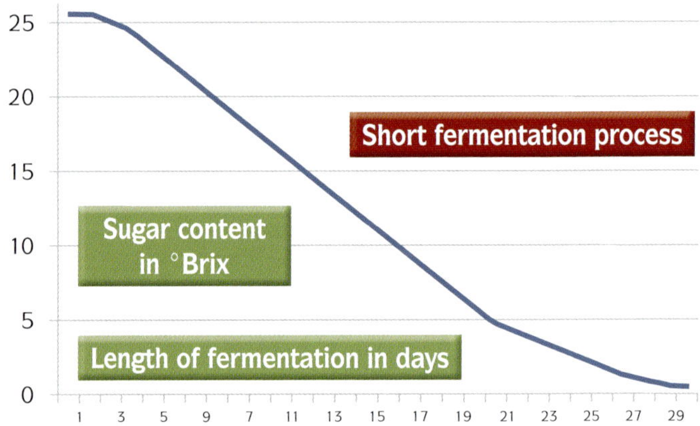

Since this method makes it possible to coordinate the mead batches by taste, it is appreciated by enterprises that brew mead as a separate line of business.

Primary product

In brewing mead, the basic liquid is either water or fruit juice, or a fruit juice-water mixture. What basic liquid you use, of course, has just as big an impact on creating the flavor as the choice of honey. If you want to produce classical pure honey wine, the choice will be water. Otherwise, the pure honey taste will be more or less affected, depending on the proportion of fruit juice. If you replace the water completely with apple juice, for example—strictly speaking—the end product will not be honey wine, but rather a honey-fruit wine, or honey wine with fruit juice.

Water

Old recipes require "soft" water, i.e., water with a low lime content, and therefore recommend using rain water. For hygienic reasons (bird droppings, dust, pollutants) it is no longer advisable today to use rainwater to brew mead.

Since a mead producer has only a limited choice of water, normally he has to fall back on any normal tap water which meets Primary Drinking Water Regulations. Using distilled water is not recommended, since this water is only approved for technical use (irons, car batteries...) and is not classified for human consumption.

After a number of trials at the Warth Beekeeping School, we became aware that the choice of the water has only a limited effect on the final quality.

Clean fermentation and careful processing up to bottling are much more important than the choice of water.

Fruit juice

Using fruit juice as a basic liquid not only affects the taste, but also how the fermentation behaves. Since freshly squeezed fruit juices contain pulp, and thus inherent yeast nutrients such as nitrogen and phosphorus compounds and vitamins, there is no need to add these nutrients separately. Often, mixing an already fermenting fruit juice, to which pure culture yeast was previously added, into the honey-water mixture caused fermentation to start more quickly.

Red fruit juices give the mead a reddish color, such as using cherry or sour cherry juice to make "Viking blood."

The fruit acid in the juice is another advantage. Aciditiy is an important ingredient, not only for taste balance but also for the mead's longevity.

This can partly save adding more acidity to the mead starter.

Advantages of using fruit juice as basic liquid:

- fewer fermentation problems
- fermentation starts quicker
- higher acidity

Honey

In principle, all types of honey are suitable for brewing mead. However, since brewing mead should be a processing enterprise, it is advisable to use honey that is available in larger amounts and gets a low sale price.

It does not make economic sense to process wild honey, since this enjoys a strong demand on the market and achieves a high sales price.

It is also possible to use problem honey—with too high a water content or once overheated—to make mead, after proper pretreatment. For adjusting residual sugar after fermentation, the choice of honey is especially important. Here, you should use honey that will give the mead its typical aroma. Intensely flavored blossom honeys are recommended.

An already fermenting honey cannot be used for this purpose, since the start of fermentation gives the honey a slightly acidic sting, which has an unpleasant effect on the mead.

In conclusion, some honeys for making mead:

Linden honey

This is one of the most aromatic honeys. The bittersweet note is underlined with subtle citrus tones. The fragrance recalls the typical linden scent. This honey is wonderful for a dry-aged mead. The dry-aged character does not reflect the typical sweet mead, and thus appeals to lovers of sherry and such. This is a rarity, appreciated by connoisseurs.

Locust (acacia) honey

The white-flowering locust tree provides nectar for very bright-colored locust honey. The only sugar in this honey is fructose. It is not suitable to use as a single honey, because the resulting mead appears rather thin and fragile. But it is eminently suitable for mixing with other honeys.

It is particularly problematic to brew pure acacia mead. The sugar in acacia honey is a pure fructose, which is more difficult for yeast to ferment than grape sugar. Pure acacia honey is very light and low in pollen; as a result, there is little for the yeast to adhere to, and this can result in a sluggish fermentation, despite the best yeast nutrition with yeast nutrient salts. You can generally avoid these problems by using acacia honey with a pulpy fruit juice (see page 41, "Sugar").

Forest honey

In many mountain regions, this is the only honey that can be harvested—often mixed with a little blossom honey. Due to its strong, spicy and malty taste, it is also the favorite honey of most consumers. The limited harvest gives this honey a high price, which means that mead producers should start with a higher material value in their calculations. The mead it produces is consistent with these qualities, and will be a dark, very strong honey wine.

Pure grade honey wines enrich the product range.

Sunflower honey

For bees, the sunflower honey yield represents the end of their labor-intensive summer honey flow.

The resulting honey has a strong yellow color, which comes from the pollen of the flowers. Through fermentation and then clarification, the pollen falls to the bottom of the barrel and the mead appears much lighter. The aroma recalls the resinous note of sunflower honey, which is offset by the strong taste. Both for a pure mead and in a blend, this is an ideal honey for making mead.

Spring blossom honey

Early flowering plants, such as dandelion, coltsfoot, dead nettle, maple, wild cherry and the full range of fruit trees, provide nectar for this somewhat lighter, pale yellow honey. This honey is the optimal choice for classic mead. The subtle nuances of the honey, coupled with a nicely integrated acidity, will delight the palate of any mead connoisseur.

Ingredients of honey

Apart from the different sugars, such as fructose, glucose, sucrose, maltose and melezitose, which make up about 80% of the honey, it also contains about 16 to 19% water. The rest is made up of amino acids, aromatics and minerals.

What does bee honey contain?

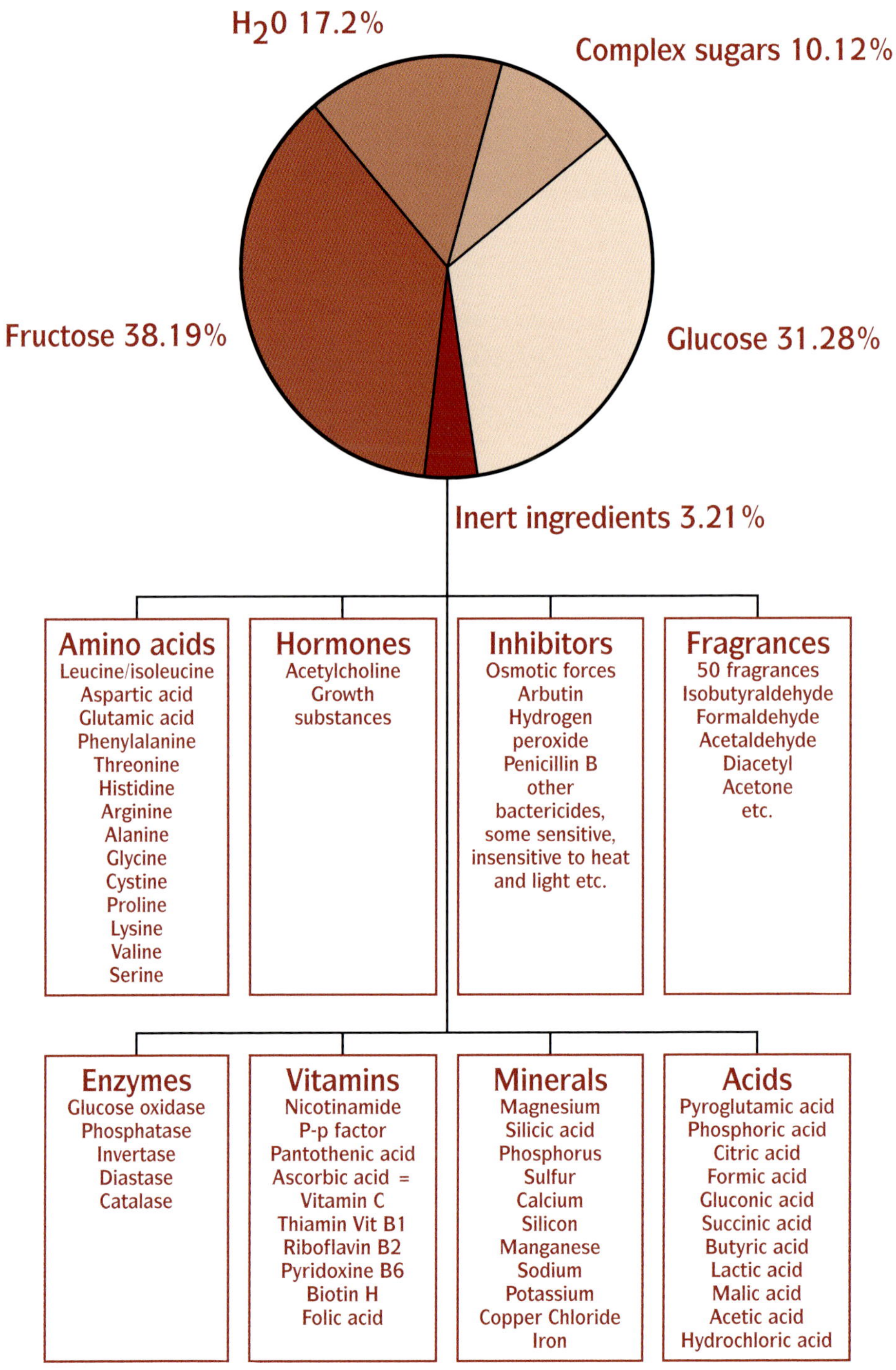

Acids

The acids contained in honey (gluconic, acetic, butyric, lactic, citric, formic, maleic and oxalic acids) do not stand out in the taste, because they are buffered and bound with minerals and sugars. However, these acids are split off in fermentation; the result is they give the fermented drink a pleasant acidic taste. When brewing mead at the Warth Beekeeping School, the water-honey mixture can have a pH value of 6.0; after fermentation is complete, we have a value of 3.3. To put it simply, this drop in pH results from splitting the sugar from the acids.

Sugar

To understand the nature of mead production, it is necessary to take a closer look at the sugar composition of honey, the starting material.

A difference from producing grape or fruit wine, where you are dealing with pure simple sugars (grape and fruit sugar), honey also contains double and multiple sugars, in addition to the simple sugars.

The proportions of glucose to fructose can vary greatly, depending on the type of honey. Pure locust honey contains only fructose, while pure rapeseed honey mainly consists of glucose. Since yeast will ferment glucose into alcohol more rapidly, fermentation problems can be more difficult in honey wines made from mostly locust honey. Fruit-loving yeasts have recently become available for sale, which were selected specifically for such situations.

Pure locust honey is difficult to ferment.

As noted, the sugar composition varies, depending on type of honey:

- Fructose 25–45%
- Glucose 20–40 %
- Sucrose up to 5%
- Maltose 4–14%
- Multiple sugar up to 15%

Multiple sugar – melezitose

A honey will have a different sugar composition, due to its source material, the nectar of various plants, or the honeydew. Thus, honeydew can have a much higher proportion of complex sugars. Melezitose honey presents big problems for the beekeeper, because it has already crystallized in the comb and cannot be spun out of the honeycomb. Multiple sugar is not fermentable. A honey that is already fermenting is not suitable for making mead. The higher the proportion of multiple sugars, the more residual sugar remains in the mead.

IMPORTANT!

Yeast can only fully ferment simple sugars. Double sugars are first decomposed into simple sugars with enzymes, and then can be fermented.

This fact is often a reason that a mead could not ferment completely – although adjusted to just 12% ABV – even if every step was taken for optimal fermentation.

Multiple sugars are not fermentable.

This residual sugar, which consists of multiple sugars – because it is not fermentable – cannot cause re-fermentation in the bottle, and thus any increased cloudiness in the honey wine is avoided.

Problem honeys

Honey with too high water content

The higher the proportion of multiple sugars, the more residual sugar remains in the mead.

Young, unripe honey can contain too much water; using it violates established regulations, and there is also the danger of fermentation in the container. It is not advisable to use it without prior heating, because this can result in faulty fermentation. Heating the honey to 158 to 176° F (70 to 80° C)(by water bath, oven, warming oven) will inactivate existing wild yeasts; then, there is nothing in the way of processing it further into mead.

HMF level is too high

Improper storage (temperature too high) can cause the HMF value (hydroxymethylfurfural) to rise above effective legal regulations. It can still be used for making mead by diluting the honey with water to make the starter, which will lower the HMF level.

Melezitose honey

Beekeepers fear a melezitose honey flow for many reasons. This flow is difficult to extract and is not liked by consumers, due to its heavy crystal formation. Melezitose honey can be melted relatively easily using a beeswax melter, and then made into mead.

Melezitose honeycombs are heated in a wax melter, liquefied, and separated from the honeycomb and wax. The honey is heated up to 194°F (90° C) in the process. Since most wax melters work using water vapor, this also increases water enrichment (up to about 25% water content).

The hot, thin melezitose honey is strained and can now easily be processed into mead; water is used to get it to the desired sugar concentration, pure culture yeast and yeast nutrients added, and now the honey is fermented.

The method of leaching melezitose honey out of the combs by putting them in warm water for several hours cannot be used, due to the high risk of spontaneous fermentation or bacterial infection.

For hygienic reasons, only unhatched combs may be processed.

Results of heating:

- kills foreign yeasts
- gives the honey and resulting mead an interesting malty tone
- the malted sugar gives the mead a more intense brown color
- all valuable ingredients are inactivated
- the mead gets a broad malty note.

Since other uses melezitose honey are labor-intensive as well as questionable (feeding livestock), the method described above is best.

Melezitose honeycomb (left). The hot honey-wax mixture flows out (right).

Work steps - Mead starter

1. Calculate honey needed
2. Hot water
3. Stir in warmed honey
4. Fill with cold water
5. Determine sugar content
6. Calculate alcohol
7. Prepare for fermentation
8. Monitor the fermentation

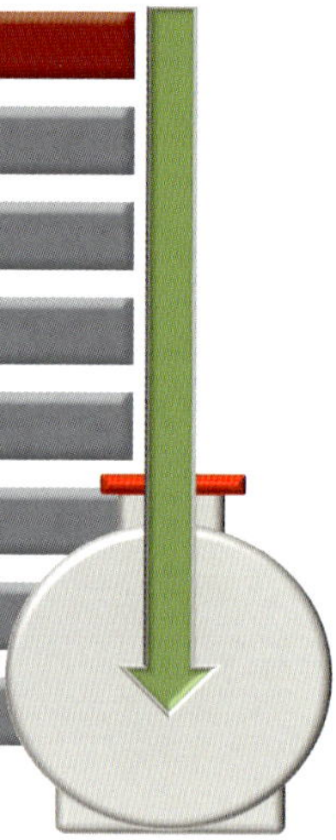

Calculating your honey requirement

Brewing mead is much easier if the brewer can use a short calculation to determine how much honey is needed for the starter solution. This way, the mead brewer can know exactly how much honey he needs if, for example, he wants to brew 200 liters of mead with a desired 14% ABV.

The brewer will use more or less honey depending on whether the goal is mead with a higher or lower alcohol and residual sugar content.

Using these simple calculations, we can calculate:

- how much honey is needed for the mead starter, and
- what the approximate final alcohol content will be after complete fermentation.

These are benchmark calculations, and not scientifically exact, since they are based on educated guesses, but will work in practice. They were devised in metric terms.

To make these calculations, you need the following information:

1. There is about 750 g fermentable sugar per 1 kg of honey, a ratio of 0.75 sugar to 1 honey.
2. 1 kg of honey absorbs about 0.7 liters sugar.
3. 1 quart (1 liter) of apple juice contains an average of 3.53 oz (100 g) sugar.

First, the mead brewer should be clear about what calculated final alcohol content he wants from his mead starter solution. In the example cited above, the beekeeper wants to brew 200 liters of mead with a 14% ABV final alcohol content.

Honey requirement calculation

14% ABV	x	19*	=	266	x	200	=	53200	÷	800	=	66.5
desired alcohol content		fixer factor		necessary fermentable sugar in 1 liter in grams		200 liters prepared starter		total sugar requirement for 200 liters in grams		approx. sugar content of 1 kg honey in grams		approximate honey requirement in kg for 200 liters with 14% ABV

* *Fixer factor: To yield 1% ABV, about 19 g fermentable sugar are needed (in theory, 17 g – in practice, the amount works out to 19 g).*

For 200 liters prepared mead starter, you would need about 66.5 kg honey to obtain about 14% ABV after complete fermentation of the sugar.

If you want to obtain 16% ABV, instead of 14%, calculate as follows:

16% ABV	x	19*	=	304	x	200	=	60800	÷	800	=	76
desired alcohol content		fixer factor		necessary fermentable sugar in 1 liter, in g		liters prepared starter		total sugar requirement for 200 liters in g		approx. sugar content of 1 kg honey in g		honey requirement in lbs for 200 liters with 16% ABV

For 200 liters mead starter, you require about 76 kg honey. This mixture would, theoretically, yield about 16% ABV after complete fermentation of the sugar. Since you could not get a 16% ABV using a "normal" yeast, this means that you will have a more or less large amount of residual sugar left over, depending on the degree of fermentation.

After fermentation ends, if you determine, for example, there is a 12.5% ABV, you can calculate the possible residual sugar level, using a rough calculation as follows:

16% ABV	-	12% ABV	=	3.5% ABV	x	19	=	66.6 g
alcohol content, possible by calculation		alcohol content yield in % ABV		alcohol left over in the form of sugar		fixer factor		approximate residual sugar content in 1 liter of mead

Thus, this would produce a mead with 12.5% ABV and 66 g of residual sugar per quart. This would not be a particularly sweet product, and to ensure longevity it should be bottled "warm" (see the chapter on "Bottling," starting on page 86).

Final alcohol content calculation

Just as above, we can reverse the calculation to find the potential final alcohol content.

Take an old recipe according to Herold, which calls for 100 l of water and 37.5 kg of honey. In this case, it should be noted that the 37.5 kg of honey is dissolved in 100 l of water, and thus yields more volume.

				Volume in quarts (liters)
37.5 kg honey	x	**0.7**	=	**26.25**
100 l water				**100.00**
Total volume in quarts (liters}				**126.25**

The potential final alcohol content (with full fermentation) can be calculated as follows:

37.5 kg	x	800	=	30000	÷	126.25	=	237	÷	19	=	12.4
(35 oz) honey		approx. sugar content in 1 kg honey in g		total sugar content in g		liters prepared mead starter		approx. sugar content in 1 l mead starter in g		fixer factor		kg potential alcohol content in % ABV.

This honey-water mixture, fermented using a vigorously fermenting yeast, yields about 12.4% ABV.

If you were to mix the 37.5 kg of honey with water, to get a total of 100 l mead starter solution, you would come to a potential alcohol content of

30000:100 liters = 300:19 = 15.7% ABV

The calculation serves as a basis for the starter.

There are many variable factors which can affect these calculations; the values obtained can only provide a reference point, in the search for the ideal proportions for mead.

If the mead is prepared before fermentation to yield a higher alcohol content (e.g. 19% ABV), then you should proceed with a slow fermentation process. It can take several months, due to the high sugar concentration which makes fermentation difficult.

It is possible you will not obtain the calculated alcohol content, since yeast is sensitive to alcohol, and fermentation will stop at about 12 to 14% ABV – the remaining sugar gives a residual sweetness.

By using special yeasts, which are cultivated to produce a particularly high alcohol level, it is possible to get an alcohol content of up to about 17% ABV.

The above calculation only serves to let you determine, beforehand, how much honey will be processed.

It is essential to accurately determine the sugar in the starter honey-water solution. This allows us to accurately calculate the potential alcohol content.

Dissolving the honey

If you want to preserve the honey's valuable ingredients, do not heat the honey and honey-water mixture any higher than 113° F (45° C), at most. This preserves the valuable ingredients, but also increases the risk that harmful organisms in the honey will grow during fermentation, making the product un-drinkable.

To avoid this risk (usually for larger amounts of mead), you can heat the honey using a honey-melting device to 158-176° F (70-80° C). This will inactivate the mead-damaging bacteria and yeasts already in the honey, and decrease the likelihood that the mead will be spoiled by a faulty fermentation.

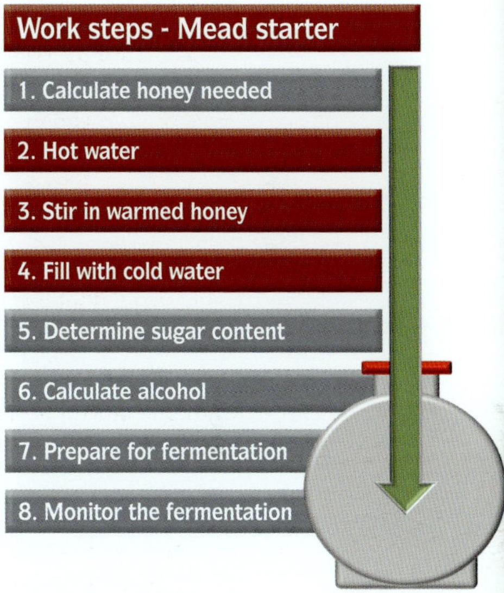

In old recipes, we often find instructions to boil the honey-water mixture so long that a hen's egg can float in it; but there is no purpose to this boiling from the perspective of microbiology and fermentation technique. Of course, it will kill off all pests. We can also achieve this in a shorter heating time: heating to158° F (70° C) for a few minutes is sufficient. However, since it is not easy to cool the honey rapidly, it should not be exposed to heat for any longer than absolutely necessary.

There is no additional benefit from cooking the honey-water mixture for a long time.

WAYS TO PREPARE HONEY	
Heat the honey to 104° F (40° C), then mix with water	■ Maintains valuable ingredients ■ Lower risk of faulty fermentation
Heat the honey to 158° F (70° C); then mix with water	■ Honey dissolves easily ■ Easy procedure ■ Lower risk of faulty fermentation due to microorganisms ■ Ingredients are destroyed
Heating the entire honey-water mixture	■ Technically complicated and not efficient ■ Possible in small amounts ■ Heat-sensitive protein will be eliminated

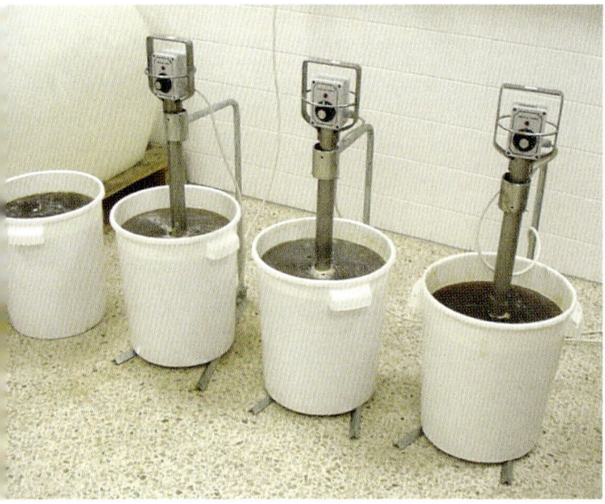

Heating the honey using a honey melter

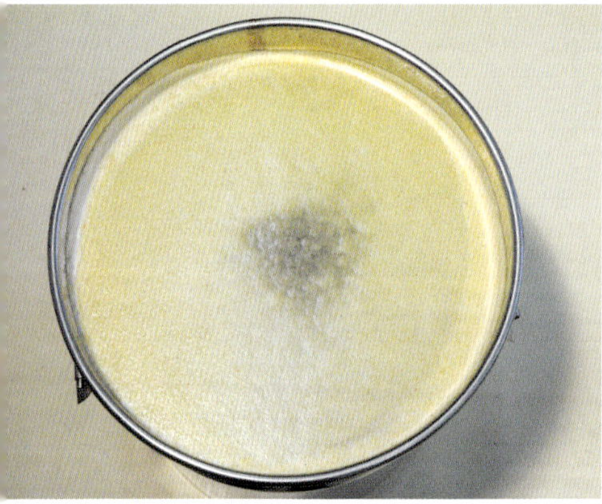

Bits of wax and foam particles accumulate on the surface; these are skimmed off with a spatula.

Stir in the warmed and measured honey

Determining the amount of sugar in the starter solution

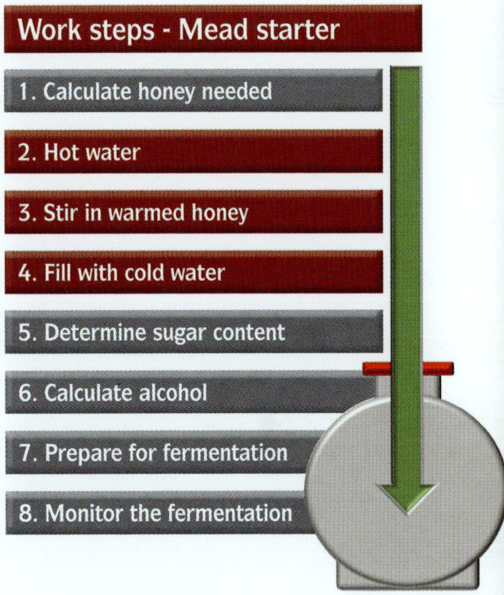

The sugar content can be stated in different units:

°Oe (degree Oechsle)

This is the most common unit to indicate the sugar content and give the relative density of the measured liquid. It is read in abbreviated form. The Oechsle scale registers 78° for a mead starter solution with a relative density of 1.078.

> Degrees Oechsle x 0.13 = potential alcohol content

°Brix (degrees Brix scale)

In the U.S., Canada, and France, the "Brix" scale degree is the most-used unit to indicate sugar content; it gives the sugar content in weight percentage.

> °Brix x 0.585 = potential alcohol content

Specific Gravity

In the U.K. and elsewhere, specific gravity is used unit to indicate sugar content; 1 gram of sugar per liter yields a specific gravity of 1.

> Specific gravity x 13 = potential alcohol content

There are two ways of measuring to determine the sugar content:

Saccharometer
(sugar spindle, sugar scale, must scale, Oechsle scale)

As you can see, there are many terms for one and the same measurement method. The lower the density of a liquid, i.e. the less sugar in the mead starter solution, the deeper the "sugar scale" sinks.

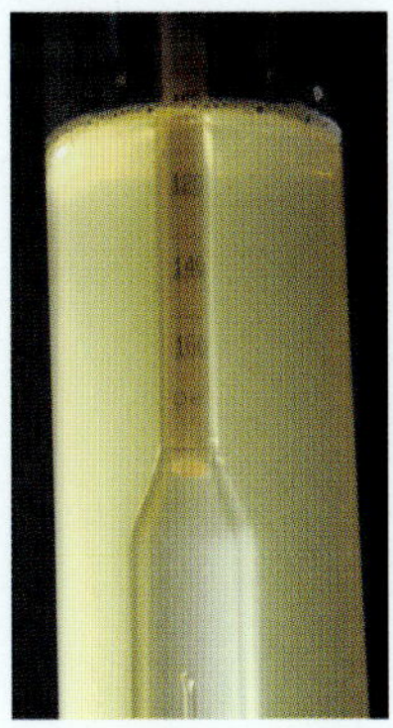

A sugar scale should be read from "below."

To determine sugar using a "sugar scale," note the following:

- The sugar scale must be clean and dry.
- The mead starter should not be fermenting yet.
- The temperature of the mead starter, must match the temperature for which the scale is calibrated
- Read the spindle correctly (whether this should be from above or below, is indicated on the sugar scale). If there is no information on how to read the scale, it is from the bottom!

Fill a clean glass cylinder with the measured mead starter. Now, slowly lower the spindle into the cylinder, without touching the side. Using a slight twist and then extracting it will remove any adhering gas bubbles. After it has settled, you can read the measuring spindle.

Mead starter with stirrer and refractometer

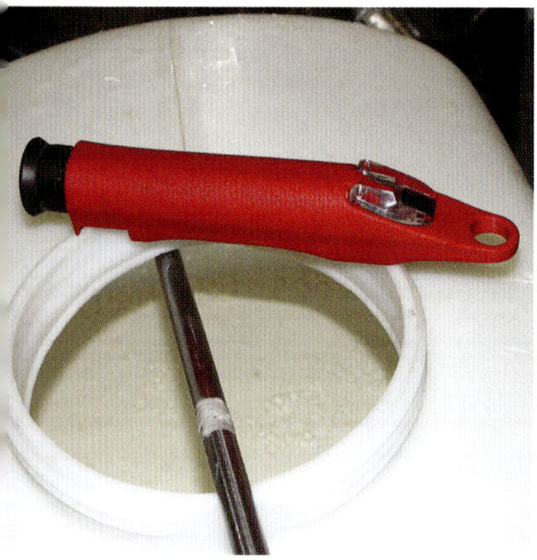

Refractometer

Here, the measurement principle is based on refraction of light. The less sugar concentration in the liquid, the more sharply the light is deflected. Brush the prism surface with 2 to 3 drops (average sample) and close the cover. Aim it at a light source, and then read off the sugar content through the eyepiece, on the light-shadow boundary. Calibrate the refractometer using distilled water at 68° F (20° C). For easier operation, we recommend a refractometer with temperature compensation, otherwise you must bring the mixture to be tested to the temperature for which it is calibrated. The refractometer is significantly more expensive than a sugar scale.

Summary of work steps:

STEP 1	STEP 2	STEP 3	STEP 4	STEP 5
Calculate amounts of honey and water	Dissolve the honey in water	Measure the honey in honey-water mixture	Calculate the potential final alcohol content	Make any necessary corrections

Preparing for fermentation

One of the most important phases of brewing mead is preparing for fermentation. This involves procedures which cannot be reversed –a point which critically influences the later quality of the mead.

Preparing for fermentation includes:

- Converting to acid
- Adding yeast nutrient salts
- Using pure culture yeast

Goals of fermentation preparation:

- Rapid start of fermentation within 12 hours
- Brisk fermentation
- Clean fermentation
- High alcohol yield

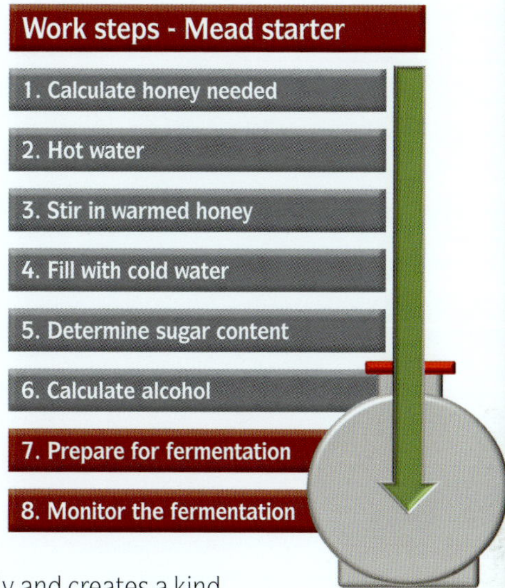

Acidification

As stated in the chapter on "Honey selection," honey contains many different acids, which are released through the fermentation process. Despite this variety of acids, the quantity is not enough to achieve a balanced taste and to resist harmful microorganisms.

Converting to an acid is done for two reasons:

- The sensory evaluation will be more positive.
- To lower the pH value, which occurs simultaneously and creates a kind of acid protection, i.e., the fermenting liquid and the mead are better protected from any attack from harmful organisms.

A beverage's acidity is given in grams/liter or parts per thousand. The higher the acidity, the better a beverage will keep. When considering increasing acidity, it is important to strike the right balance between acid protection and creating balanced flavor. Adding too much acid will make the mead scratchy and give it an unpleasant sharpness.

What to watch for:

- Only use citric acid that is specifically intended for the wine making trade.
- 100 g of citric acid per 100 l, increase acidity by 1 part per thousand.
- Fermented mead, if not acidified, contains about 3 to 4 parts per thousand.
- The goal is a value around 6 parts per thousand.
- Citric acid is first dissolved in a little mead and then stirred well.

To round off the flavor, you can also acidify the mead after fermentation. In Germany, you may add a maximum of 3 g of citric acid (and no more) per liter of mead. In Austria, lactic and malic acids may also be used.

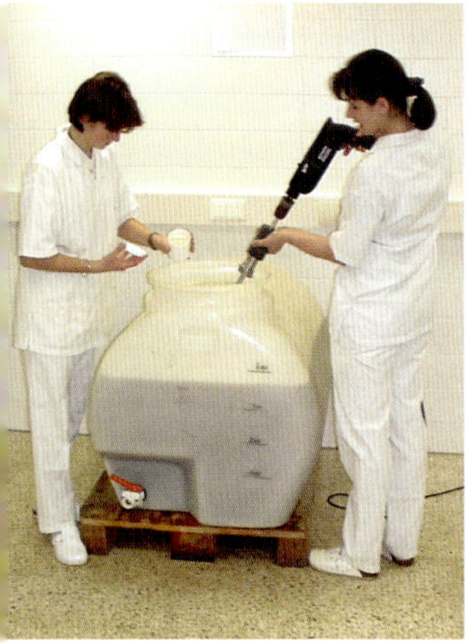

Stirring in the dissolved yeast nutrients.

Yeast nutrient salts

Nitrogen and phosphorus compounds and B group vitamins serve as food for the yeast cells. Honey contains very few yeast nutrients of these groups, so "feeding" the yeast is essential to ensure brisk fermentation.

You can buy simple yeast nutrient salts, composed of nitrogen and phosphorus, but complex nutrients are also available, which, in our case, are preferable. These consist of ammonium sulfate, di-ammonium phosphate and thiamine.

The amounts to use are from 30 to 50 g per 100 liters, depending on the product. We recommend that you use the amounts specified on the product or product information sheet.

Dissolve the weighed yeast nutrients in a little warm water and stir in before the yeast is added.

Pure culture yeast

Fermentation is a biochemical process: sugar is converted into alcohol and carbon dioxide is released in the process. Fermentation creates other by-products, both positive and negative. This biochemical process releases heat.

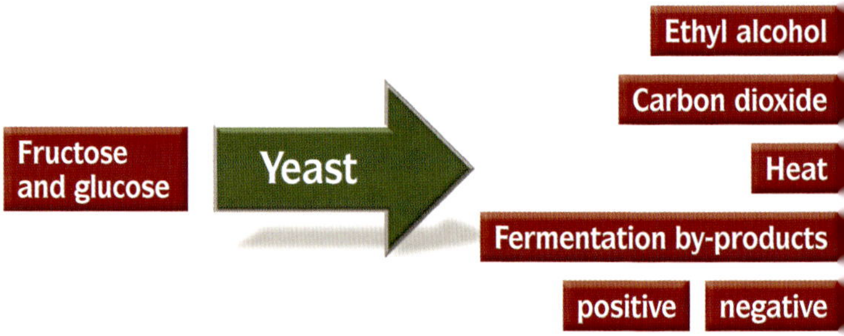

The decomposition of sugar into alcohol shown in this schematic representation, actually occurs in many small, individual reactions. This is not particularly important for anyone making wine. What is much more important, is that he know what affects fermentation, and what conditions must be created, to ensure that fermentation goes cleanly and keeps going, without stopping.

View of a fermentation tank

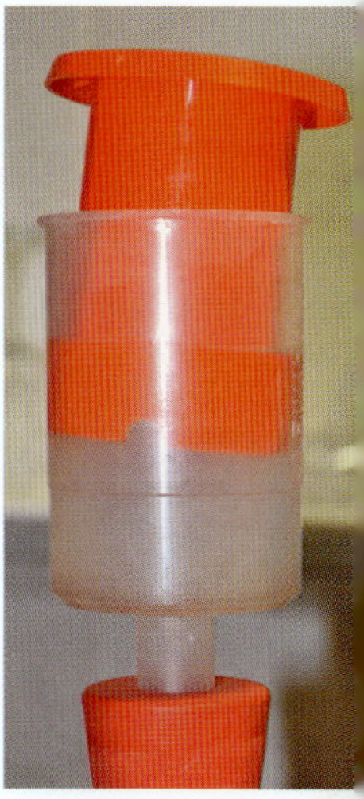

Fermentation tube, filled with water

We want fermentation that:

- Begins rapidly,
- Proceeds rapidly without stopping,
- Makes little foam
- Produces few undesired fermentation by-products ("clean" fermentation) and
- Yields a high alcohol content.

We achieve this by:

- Adding yeast nutrients
- Using pure culture yeast
- Filling the fermentation container to 90% full and sealing it with a fermentation bung
- Fermentation temperature between 64.4 - 68° F (18-20° C).

Yeast selection

In many recipes you can find references to using **liquid yeasts** such as sherry, port wine, samos, malaga, etc. These liquid yeasts were the forerunners of today's dry, pure culture yeasts. The cell count of liquid yeasts is so low that, before you add it to the mead starter solution you have to use a fermentation starter, i.e., pre-fermenter. The process is laborious and the results of fermentation are not satisfactory.

Liquid yeasts are not recommended.

Use of dry pure culture yeast is a standard, modern wine-making technique. There are yeasts for every specific purpose: special strains of yeast for making white, red and sparkling wines, as well as to ferment mashes for distilling.

To ferment honey, with its own special requirements, vigorously fermenting and alcohol-tolerant yeast strains such as saccharomyces bayanus have proven their value.

This yeast strain is available from any yeast supplier; the supplier can give you professional advice on how to find the yeast most suitable for your enterprise. Product names include: Oenoferm Freddo, Anchor N96, Bioferm killer, Filtraferm bayanus, etc.

Yeasts are unicellular and classified in the kingdom fungi.

"Killer yeasts" are a special type of yeast. If you don't heat either the honey or the honey-water mixture, to protect the valuable ingredients, then using a "killer yeast" lessens the risk of faulty fermentation. These yeasts start fermentation rapidly and also can eliminate wild yeasts, which are more common in unheated honeys, by creating toxins.

However, there is no absolute guarantee that this will prevent faulty fermentation.

How much and how to add it

Because mead is difficult to ferment, you should use an amount between 20 to 30 g/100 liters. Do not add the weighed yeast directly to the starter; it must be rehydrated beforehand. To do this, stir the measured yeast into 10 times the amount of warm water, at 95° to 104° F (35° to 40° C), and let it stand for 10 minutes. Afterwards, add a small amount of mead starter solution, stir it in, and let the starter rest again for 10 minutes. A foam layer forms during this time and the yeast is now ready for use. This step-by-step rehydration process makes the yeast cell walls permeable for the sugar.

NOTE:

- Don't add the yeast to water that is any cooler or warmer than the stated 95° to 104° F (35-40° C)!
- Don't leave the yeast in the solution for any longer than 20 minutes!

Rehydrating yeast for 21 quarts (20 liters) of mead starter solution

***Figure 1**:* *Have 50 ml of water at 100° F (38° C).*

***Figure 2**:* *Stir in 4 g of yeast.*

***Figure 3**:* *Let stand for maximum 10 minutes.*

***Figure 4**:* *Stir in 50 ml of mead starter.*

***Figure 5**:* *After it stands for another 10 minutes, the yeast starter forms a crown of foam; now you can stir it into the mead.*

In our experience, the following procedures give the best results:

1. Heat the honey to 104° F (40° C). (Exception: If the honey has a water content over 19% – heating to 158° F (70° C) is recommended).

Heating

2. Fill the fermentation tanks with hot tap water.

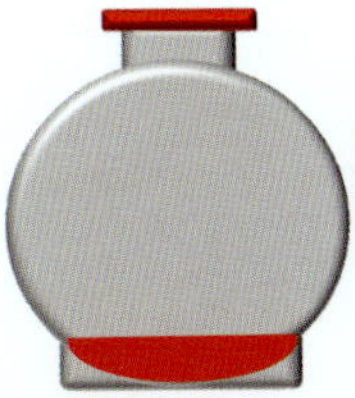

A maximum of 1/4 full with hot water

3. Mix in and dissolve the warmed honey.

Stir in honey

4. Fill the fermentation tank with cold water to reach the desired sugar content level. It is necessary to measure sugar concentration frequently. Meanwhile, this cools the solution to about 68° to 77° F (20° to 25° C).

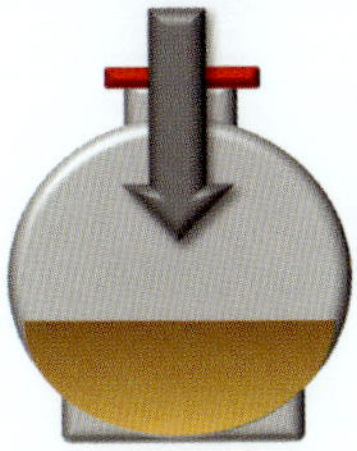

Fill with cold water

5. Other steps to prepare for fermentation include acidification, adding yeast nutrients, and the rehydrated pure culture yeast.

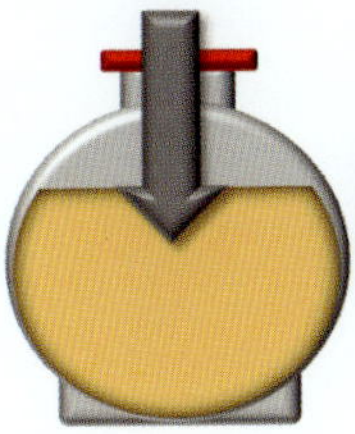

Prepare for fermentation

Fermentation

Fermentation fundamentally changes the entire beverage. In several stages, sugar is converted into alcohol, acids are released, and byproducts such as carbon dioxide, acetaldehyde and others, are formed.

Monitoring the fermentation process includes:

- Temperature control (at least 59° F [15° C], max 77° F (25° C) – ideal: 64.5° F [18° C]
- CO_2 – development
- Constant tasting
- Changing the blocking liquid in the fermentation bell

Fermentation problems

There is a cause for each fermentation problem.

Problems with fermenting mead	Possible cause
Mead does not start to ferment	■ Did not use a pure culture yeast ■ Yeast was too old ■ Yeast solution was too hot (over 104° F (40° C)) ■ Fermentation liquid was too cold
Stuck fermentation	■ Temperature was too low ■ Lack of yeast nutrients
Fermentation goes too slowly	■ High sugar concentration ■ Fermentation temperature too low ■ Lack of yeast nutrients

If the sugar concentration is more than 29 °Brix or 125° Oe, you can expect sluggish fermentation due to the high sugar content.

Procedures after fermentation ends

Racking the lees

In contrast to wine or fruit winemaking, when you brew mead, you can only conditionally determine if fermentation has completed using the "Clinitest." In grape or fruit wines, the residual sugar content of the fermented drink will be between 1 and 10 g/liter. The Clinitest is designed for this range. In fermented mead, the residual sugar content lies between 10 to 25 g/liter.

It only makes sense to use the Clinitest when there has been a completely thorough fermentation.

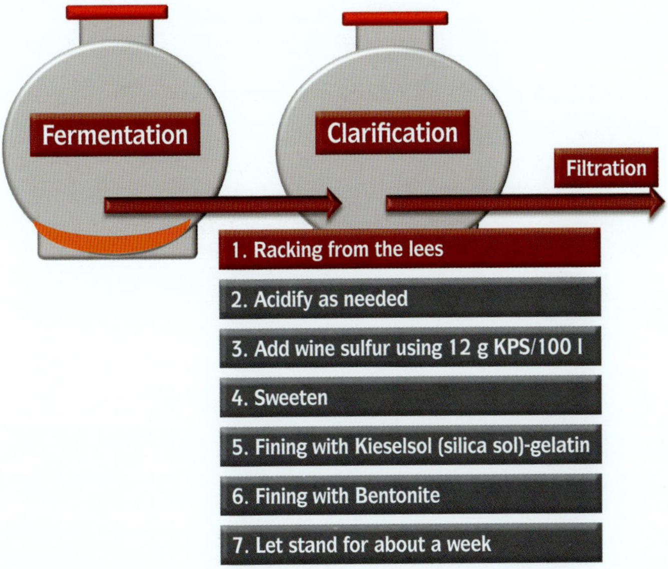

To better plan the next treatment steps, it makes sense to determine both alcohol and residual sugar levels.

This makes it possible to answer the following questions:

- How far does the actual alcohol content deviate from what you calculated?
- If the alcohol content is over 13.5% ABV, there is little risk of re-fermentation, even after sweetening.
- If the alcohol content is far below the calculated value, but there is a high residual sugar content, the fermentation is stuck.
- If the alcohol content is less than 13.5% ABV, with a low residual sugar level, re-fermentation is likely after sweetening.

Getting precise testing values makes work easier.

Failure to rack the wine off the yeast, can be the cause of many a faulty mead. Low acidity, high storage temperature and leaving some of the lees behind all create ideal conditions for the yeast to decompose — the mead will get the dreaded sulphur off-flavor. The most common disease in mead is "mousiness," caused by the preconditions for bacterial growth just described. (For particulars, see "Faults and Diseases in Mead," page 101)

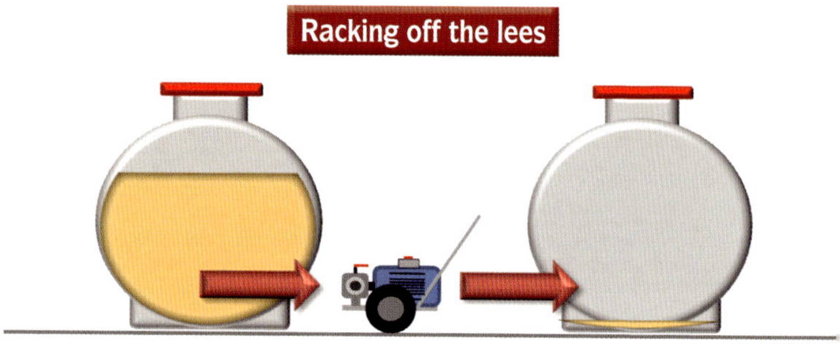

If you adjust the mead before fermentation to about 26° Brix or 110° Oe after complete fermentation of the sugar, this would yield a potential alcohol content of about 14% ABV. Primary fermentation takes 10 to 20 days. This is followed by a secondary fermentation phase, which produces less CO_2 and can take 10 to 20 days.

At what point should the mead be racked off the yeast? There are two possible scenarios:

As soon as active fermentation is finished, the mead must be drawn off the yeast dregs.

Scenario 1: Ideal case
The mead ferments rapidly for two to four weeks. The secondary fermentation phase is relatively short and ends abruptly. The mead tastes completely fermented. This would be the ideal point to rack the mead off the lees.

Scenario 2: Stuck fermentation
The mead ferments rapidly at first. After a week or so, the barrel quiets down and fermentation is sluggish. After four weeks, the mead still tastes sweet, but there is still a light fermentation going on. Even repeatedly stirring the mead starter and warming don't create the desired result.

What to do next:
In this case, it would be advisable to rack off the existing lees, and then add more yeast and yeast nutrients. If you have some mead starter already in full fermentation, this could be added. Adding some pulpy apple juice may be helpful here.

Acidification

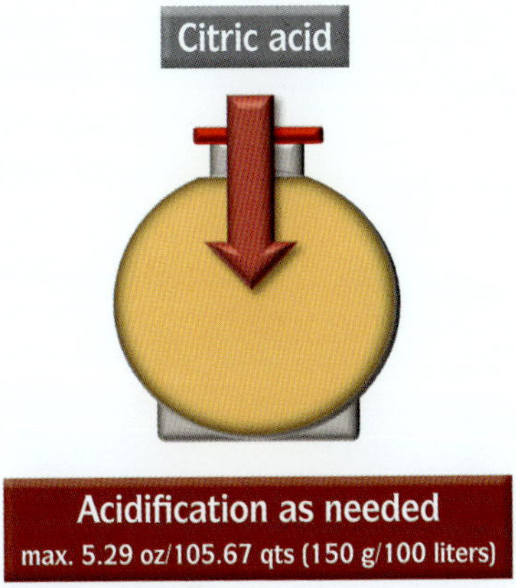

There are two parameters to use to decide if you should acidify the mead, and by how much:

- Sensory impression
- Determine the acidity

Acidity is important to give the mead a balanced taste. Acidity must not stand out too much, but should also not be completely suppressed. It is up to the brewer's discretion and sensitivity to find the right level. It is helpful to determine the acidity level, to decide what steps to take. If the mead has a total acid value below 0.176 oz/qt (5.0 g/l) (5 parts per thousand), it will be flabby and bland on the palate. Do not add any more than 5.29 oz (150 g) of citric acid per 100 qts (100 liters) after fermentation; otherwise the wine will be sharp and pungent on the palate.

Adding wine sulfur

Sulfur and its various forms have a firm place in the modern wine industry. Sulfur, in the form of potassium pyrosulfite (KPS) or potassium metabisulfite, has less of a preservative effect, but is more commonly used to prevent oxidation and all its negative effects.

If you do not add wine sulfur to the mead, it degrades quickly, turns drab in color, and is dull on the palate.

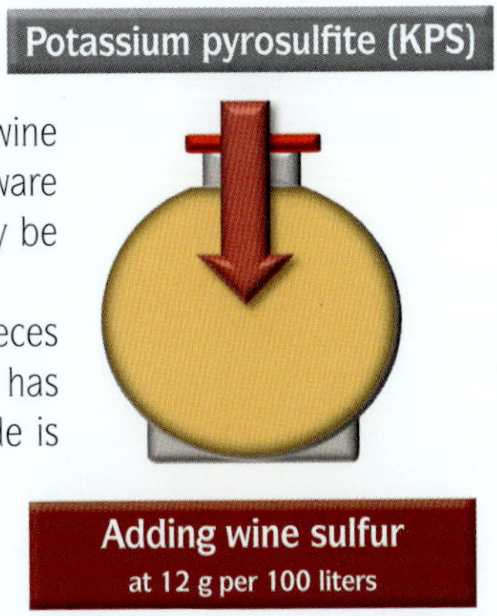

Despite intensive research, there are no substitutes available for the various effects and functions of sulfurous acid.

Sulphurous acid has proven to be an invaluable aid in wine making technique over the centuries. However, we must all be aware that this acid is harmful in larger quantities, and it should only be used on a well-informed and targeted basis.

Sulfur is applied in various forms. The best known, is using pieces of sulfur to preserve wooden barrels. One to 2% sulfurous acid has long been used as a disinfectant; currently, hydrogen peroxide is increasingly being used instead of 1 to 2% sulfurous acid.

Sulfur, in the form of potassium pyrosulfite or potassium metabisulfite, is used to add wine sulfur to honey wine.

Reasons for adding sulfur

Binding the fermentation by-product acetaldehyde

Acetaldehyde is formed during fermentation and makes the mead seem thin on the palate. In tasters' terminology, we speak of "straw like" or acrid—adding wine sulfur deals with this, making the mead firmer on the palate, with a stronger body.

Binding the oxygen dissolved in the drink, through which

- Oxidation is prevented (brown coloration) and
- A habitat for air loving microorganisms (such as acetic acid and lactic acid bacteria) is eliminated.

Form of sulfur	Commercial product	Purpose
metabisulfite ($K_2S_2O_5$) Potassium pyrosulfite (KPS) or potassium	Sulfurous acid salts Powder form 10 g or 1 kg	Adding wine sulfur to honey wine
Pure sulfur (S)	Sulfur pieces	To preserve wooden casks; in distillation, sulfur dioxide (SO_2) forms
Sulfurous acid (H_2SO_3)	5 to 6% sulfurous acid	To preserve wooden barrels and as a disinfectant, appropriately diluted
Sulfur dioxide (SO_2)	Compressed gas canisters as 100% SO_2 gas	Wood barrel preservation, also for adding sulfur to mead

Potassium pyrosulfite (KPS)

Potassium pyrosulfite is predominantly used to add sulfur to honey wines. It is available in a powder and commercially available in 1 kilogram or 10 g packages.

Before adding it to the barrel, dissolve the potassium pyrosulfite or metabisulfite in a small amount of mead, then add it to the contents of the barrel and stir thoroughly.

As already noted, do not completely rule out adding wine sulfur to honey wine.

- Add wine sulfur first during racking, at 12 g/100 liters
- Add wine sulfur a second time during aging
- Check the free sulfur shortly before bottling, and if needed, reduce the sulfur.

Weigh the potassium pyrosulfite or metabisulfite exactly.

First dissolve the potassium pyrosulfite in a little mead, then mix it in thoroughly.

Adding sulfur as potassium pyrosulfite, at 12 g/100 liters, to mead after racking will accomplish the tasks noted above.

It may be necessary to add more wine sulfur during aging, based on laboratory tests as required. The goal is to get a "free sulfur" amount of 35-40 mg/l, which should remain stable for several weeks before bottling.

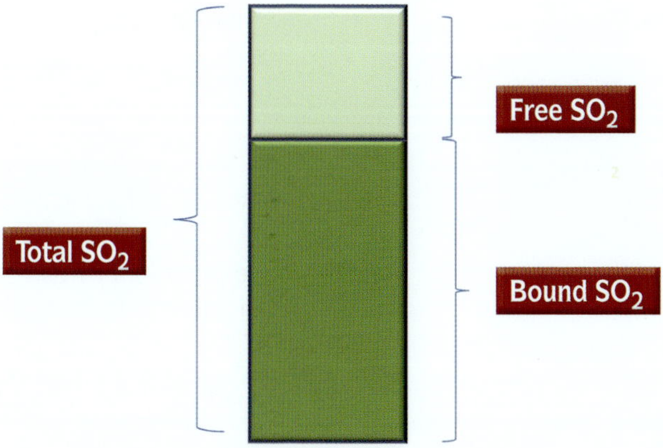

Potassium pyrosulfite is also called "KPS."

In the mead, part of the added sulfur (potassium pyrosulfite) will bind to a fermentation by-product (acetaldehyde). This is made inactive and is referred to as bound sulfurous acid. The rest stays unbound, and is callec free sulphurous acid: it gives active protection against microorganisms.

Next to acidity, a honey wine's free sulfurous acid content is an important indicator of its longevity.

$$\text{Total } SO_2 = \text{free } SO_2 + \text{bound } SO_2$$

Under Austrian wine laws, honey wine may contain no more than:

- 50 mg/l of free sulfurous acid and
- 200 mg/l sulfurous acid in total.

The goal is a free sulfurous acid content of 25-30 mg/l. If this value stays the same over a longer period, the mead can be regarded as "stable.

Adding wine sulfur

To get the desired value of 25 to 30 mg/l free sulfurous acid, it will be necessary to add sulfur during aging. You should get a test report from a wine or must consulting laboratory as a basis for this treatment.

Calculate the amount to be used as follows:

FORMULA!

Lack of free SO_2 in mg/liter x 2* =
g potassium pyrosulfite in 1,000 liters

* *Potassium pyrosulfite contains only half the active SO_2.*

Example:
Known free sulfurous acid content: 8 mg/l
Desired free sulfurous acid content: 30 mg/l
Amount lacking: 22 mg/l

Resulting calculation:
22 x 2 = 44 g of potassium pyrosulfite (KPS)/1,000 l

Sweetening – adjusting residual sugar

In the chapter titled "Description of methods," (page 33), we evaluate the advantages and disadvantages of a short fermentation period. Meac started using these methods will rapidly ferment thoroughly and appear after fermentation stops, a bit sweet, edgy and rough on the palate. It will be more like sherry than honey wine. This is certainly an interesting product, but there are few consumers for it. It is more of a raw product, a raw mead. It will only attain full balance, and the typical character of mead, if you add more honey.

Which honey should you choose to adjust the residual sugar?
If the honey you used to make the raw mead wasn't of optimal quality, (too old, high HMF level, ...), you should use a more taste-intensive honey to adjust the residual sugar level. This will give the resulting mead its characteristic odor and taste.

Only high-quality honey should be used for sweetening.

How to figure out the ideal amount of honey for sweetening?
There are three possibilities:

- Tasting
- Calculation
- A preliminary test

Tasting

The simplest method is to heat the honey 104° F (40° C) and mix it into the raw mead while stirring constantly. By tasting the mixture continuously, you can determine the ideal moment.

Calculation

For larger amounts of mead, it is important to know beforehand how much honey should be heated to add for the residual sugar. You can calculate a rough benchmark amount. As a prerequisite, you need the residual sugar content of honey wine you are sweetening in grams/liter.

Sample calculation:

110 g/l	-	15 g/l	=	95 g/l	x	120 l	=	11400 g/l	÷	800 g/l	=	14.25kg
Desired residual sugar in g/l		Existing residual sugar in g/l after end of fermentation		Lacking residual sugar in g/l		Liters of starter		Lacking sugar in 120 l mead		Sugar content in 1 kg of honey in g		Honey needed to obtain 110 g RS in 120 liters of mead

This rough calculation has proven itself very well in practice. Adding the honey increases the contents to about 130 liters (14.25 x 0.7 l = about 10 l), with the result that the honey is distributed within 130 liters; this means that the residual sugar level won't amount to the targeted 110 g, but somewhat less. But this is enough to give the brewer a rough estimate of how much honey he will need.

The honey is weighed and heated.

Immediately after the honey is addec

Preliminary tests

A most accurate, but also most expensive, method is to do a preliminary test

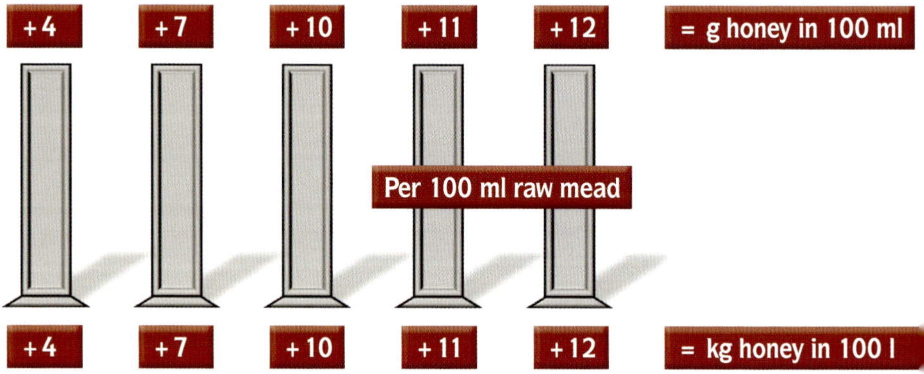

Take several 100 ml samples from the mead for sweetening: increasing amounts of honey are mixed into the samples, and then taste.

The increments used in the preliminary test depend on whether the finished mead should be more or less sweet.

> 1 kg of honey per 100 l increased the residual sugar content by about 8 grams per liter.

You can decide not only what amount of honey but also what type o honey to use, through a set of tests.

Clarification

Since consumers judge mead not only with their palate, but also their eyes, it is necessary to make a bright and stable mead.

The consumer also drinks with the eye.

By clarification, we mean removing the dregs and yeast cells.

Possible ways to clarify mead

- The mead clarifies itself
- Adding fining agents, which bond with the dregs and sink to the bottom
- Filtering cloudy honey wine

Self-clarification

The consistency of the liquid will increase, due to the existing residual sugar content.

As a result, it will be difficult to clarify the mead by filtration alone. In practice, fining beforehand has proven its value. It is highly unlikely that the mead will clarify by itself. This is most likely if fruit juices were used in the starter, since they contain the tannins necessary for clarification.

Fining

The term "fining" means adding fining agents to bond with unwanted substances. This is a purely physical process; flakes form due to charge equalization and they fall to the bottom by gravity.

For mead brewing, there are two important types of fining	
To remove the lees	A combination of Kieselsol and gelatin is used.
To remove proteins	Bentonite, a ground clay, is used.

You can consider the fining successful if the substance you want to remove (protein or lees), as well as the fining agent, are fully recovered in the fining dregs. The mead should be racked afterwards.

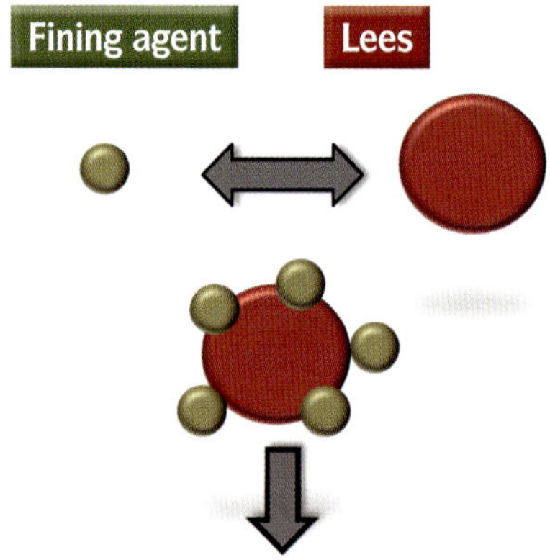

Basic prerequisites for successful fining
The mead should not be fermenting.
During fining, the mead should be at 50° F (10° C)—the warmer, the better.
Before fining, the lees resulting from fermentation must be racked from the mead.
Don't begin fining without preliminary tests!
For success, it is important that the agent is properly dispersed in the barrel. For barrels larger than 100 l, using a drill mixer is recommended.
The lower the pH value (3.8 or less), the more reactive the fining. This is also why acid should be added prior to fining.
The fining agent must be prepared exactly according to instructions (dissolve or prepare before adding).
After the fining dregs settle, the resulting dregs must be racked from the mead.

Standard fining

The various types, names and concentrations of fining agents cause the greatest difficulties for the layman. Before each usage, study the technical information sheet carefully.

In this case, it is very useful to get expert advice from wine specialty shops or information centers.

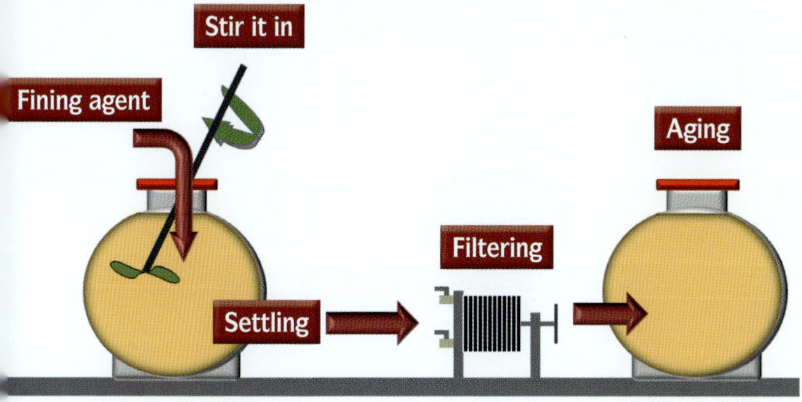

Standard fining process

(Amounts are based on 100 liters of mead)

- Stir the mead well
- Add 100 ml of 15% Kieselsol (such as Blankasit) and stir thoroughly
- Stir at least 10 minutes in intervals
- Add 50 ml of liquid gelatin (such as Gelita klar, an enzymatically decomposed liquid gelatin)
- Stir at least 10 minutes in intervals
- Add 200 g of already moistened bentonite (such as NaCalit)
- Stir at least 10 minutes in intervals
- After the fining dregs have settled to the bottom of the barrel (which will take from a few hours to one week), the mead can be racked or—even better—filtered.

Kieselsol or Silica Sol

Kieselsol is the colloidal form of silicic acid and negatively charged. It makes the components of the lees more reactive. If all the fining dregs do not settle as desired, it helps to stir the mead again, as does adding 3100 ml of silica sol.

Liquid gelatin

Gelatin is the most commonly used fining agent for wine and fruit wine making. Gelatin is made from hides; they are heated in water, releasing first the gelatin and then glue. Gelatin is frequently used in the food industry, in spreads, fruit desserts, sweets, and so on. Gelatin for fining is available in powdered and liquid form, but also combined with casein and isinglass.

Fining to remove lees (70 ml liquid gelatin and 150 ml 15% silica sol per 100 l mead)

Powdered gelatin must be liquefied prior to use. Liquid gelatin is preferred for mead brewing, since it eliminates this preparatory step, which must be done very carefully.

Bentonite

Unlike fining with silica sol and gelatin, which are used to bind to the lees, bentonite is primarily used to bind with the protein dissolved in the liquid. Bentonite also binds with the fine lees as a side effect, and forms a compact lees deposit. The legal maximum amount is 400 g/100 l; normally, 200 g is sufficient.

Bentonite is a finely ground recycled clay, which is available in granulated form and must be dissolved before use.

Slowly add the weighed amount of bentonite into 5- to 7-times the amount of water, while stirring constantly. After a few hours, the bentonite settles to the bottom and the water lying above it can be drawn off and discarded. Mix the bentonite, now lump-free, with a little mead and add to the barrel contents, while stirring constantly.

Mixing in the weighed amount of bentonite.

After 4-6 hours, the water is removed and the dissolved bentonite mixed into the barrel.

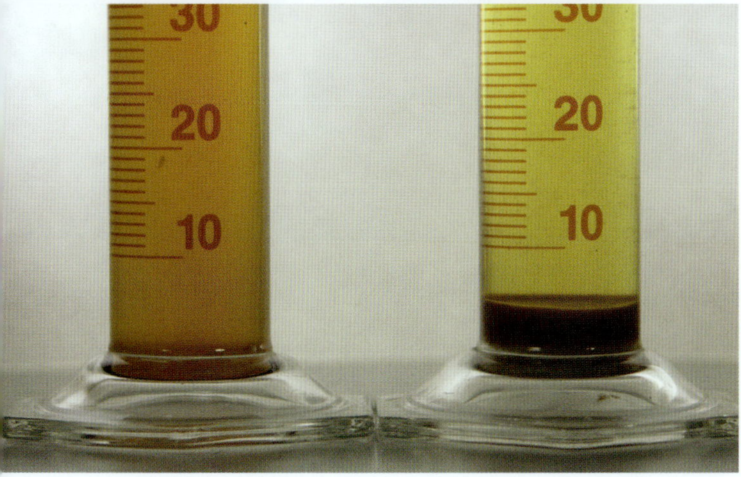

The result: without fining (left) and a successful fining with compact fining lees (right)

Racking the fining lees with simultaneous filtration

If it is possible to use a filter, this is the optimal solution. Carefully siphon off the mead from the already fined barrel, up to the top of the fining lees. Any siphoned lees will stick in the filter. The mead in the new barrel will be completely clear.

Racking the fining lees without filtering

If there is no possibility of filtering the mead, it can be carefully racked from the fining lees. If some fining lees are also siphoned off, this will later settle to the barrel bottom. After a few weeks, do another racking to separate the mead from these particles. There is no guarantee that the product will be completely clear.

Filtration

You also drink with your eyes—a clear product speaks for itself.

It is highly unlikely that the mead will clarify by itself. After the fining described above, we are already much closer to the goal. Anyone who wants to sell their mead will have to filter it. Here are some more-or-less appropriate methods:

The funnel filter

This is offered in many catalogs for the hobby winemaker, but it can't deliver what it promises. The amount that can be filtered at one time is small and the filtering is insufficient, which exasperates the mead brewer.

TIP

Don't spend the money for a funnel filter, but invest in a somewhat more expensive plate filter.

The candle filter

The candle filter

The mead is pressed through a filter cartridge via a pump. The filter cartridges are available with different pore sizes. This type of filtration is particularly suitable for the final filtration before bottling. The cartridges can be re-used after thorough flushing with water and soaking in a preservative solution.

The plate filter

Filters based on the principle of filtering through layers are the most frequently used in making fruit and grape wines. Equipment for this type of filtration is relatively large, but there are devices that can be used for our type of application, which are smaller and therefore less expensive. These can also be used to filter liqueurs, brandies, and grape and fruit wines.

The product to be filtered is pressed through cellulose layers, so that the lees are trapped in and on the layers. The mead comes out of the filter free of lees.

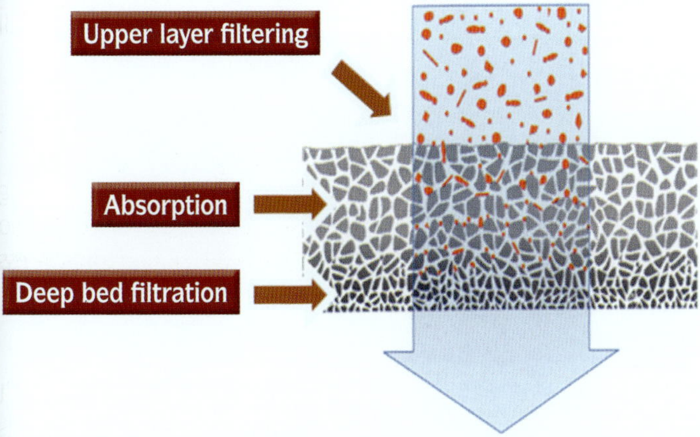

How a filter membrane works (Sketch by Fa. Begerow)

How finely the mead will be filtered depends on the choice of filter membranes. Coarser membranes are used for products that are very cloudy; you only get clear mead if you do a further fine filtration. Sterilization membranes are so dense, that they even filter out microorganisms. To do this, you must do a pre-filtration using a fine filter. Sterile filtration is done during bottling.

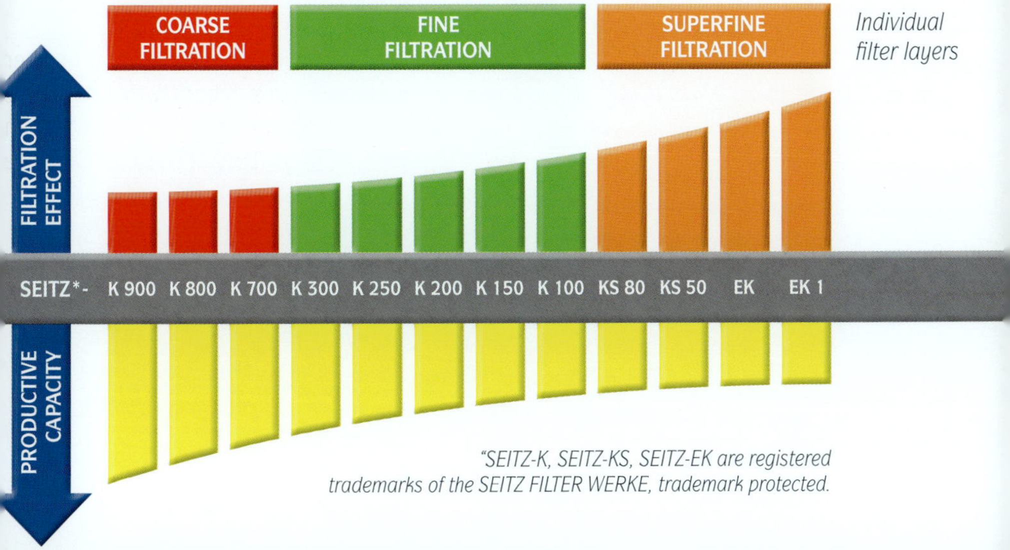

Individual filter layers

SEITZ-K, SEITZ-KS, SEITZ-EK are registered trademarks of the SEITZ FILTER WERKE, trademark protected.

A round plate filter with hand pump for small quantities (left)
Plate filter 30/30 cm with impeller pump (right)

Filter membrane manufacturers produce their own summary tables showing designation, filtration efficiency and capacity. Unfortunately, these designations vary from one manufacturer to another.

Rinsing

Since the filter membranes are made of cellulose, it is necessary to soak them before the actual filtration. First insert the membranes in the filter and then pump water through, leaving them taste-neutral. You can only start filtering after this procedure; if it is omitted, or not thorough enough, the honey wine will have a papery taste.

Rinsing the filter membranes until they are taste-neutral.

Aging

You can age the mead for a longer period in the barrel, if you have eliminated any risk that fermentation will restart and the mead is stable.

For longer aging, the mead should meet the following criteria:

Criterion	Effect
Fill barrel completely	Prevents oxidation and premature aging
Alcohol content should be at least 12.5% ABV; better at 13.0% ABV.	Impedes renewed fermentation
The mead should be stored after a fine filtering	Reduces cell and germ count – impedes spoilage by microorganisms
Acidity should be checked and increased as needed	A lower pH level will protect against microorganisms
A "free sulfur" content of 30-40 mg/l is ideal	This requires adding wine sulfur in the form of potassium pyrosulfite at 10 g per 100 l.

Preparing for bottling

The mead has been sweetened, wine sulfur added, clarified, and filtered. Now it is aging in the barrel and ready for bottling. This is the time you can make some corrections.

Blending

It is an advantage for any mead brewer to have several batches of honey wine on hand. This opens up many more possibilities to make fine adjustments to the mead before bottling it. Blending two or more honey wines creates a lot of potential to improve quality. For example, a wine with too much residual sugar can be balanced by blending the wine with a drier mead.

BASIC RULE Do not blend without a preliminary test!

Flavoring

Flavorings – spices and herbs – have a chapter of their own in mead brewing. Since time immemorial, spices and herbs have been added, often because these can cover up any side effects of any mildly faulty fermentation.

For today's consumer, there is a very clear difference between a classic mead, in which the taste and fragrance of honey dominate, and honey wine with flavorings and/or fruit juices. These are a separate category, and are difficult to compare with classic honey wine.

There is a broad range of possibilities for anyone who wants to make a spiced mead or mead with fruit juices to find a fine, balanced blend of flavorings. Old textbooks provide a lot of information on the variety of flavorings. Commonly used spices or herbs include: rosemary, nutmeg, lemon balm, wormwood, hops, ginger, and cloves. Here, you can give your imagination a free rein.

In addition to the composition of flavorings, other factors play a role, including:

- When they are added
- How they are added

When to add spices and herbs

The flavoring, or combination of flavorings, can be added either before or after fermentation, during aging, or just before bottling. The longer the flavoring is in the mead, the more balanced the blend. However, if the time is too long, there is a risk that the impact of the flavor will be too intense.

How to add spices and herbs

- **Add the flavorings directly to the starter**

  Add the seasonings (dried herbs) to the mead starter solution before fermentation starts.

  Advantage: The seasonings have enough time to affect the mead. They are removed by racking the wine off the lees.

  Disadvantage: It is hard to control the exact amount for flavor intensity.

- **Add the seasonings in linen bags**
  Tie the selected herbs and spices into a little linen bag and add it to the mead to steep. This can be done at any time during mead brewing.
  Advantage: Constant tasting will let you determine when to remove the linen bags.

- **Adding herbal extracts**
  Chop the herbs and flavorings and add to an approximately 50% to 60% alcohol solution. Let the aromatics infuse into the alcohol solution; then filter the mixture, which now can be used for seasoning.
  Advantage: It is possible to add an exact amount, even to the already fermented drink.

- **Adding essences**
  Natural extracts and essences can be produced at home or purchased from specialty companies. Since these specialty companies make only such products, they have good experience and the range of their offerings is correspondingly large.
  Advantage: You can get many different flavors and it is possible to add an exact amount.

Coloring

The popular image of mead includes:

- Mead is sweet
- Tastes like honey
- Has a darker color and
- Is high in alcohol

Sugar levels that are too-high and with too much seasoning are considered objectionable and even repellent. People often do not associate any very bright color with mead, like honey wines made from rapeseed and locust honeys.

The darker the drink, the better the consumer will consider the quality.

A producer has three ways to give mead a darker color and a more pleasing appearance:

- Add caramel
- Add dye plants or plant parts
- Add colorful juices

Caramel

Caramel can be made at home at any time. Heat some granulated sugar in a skillet over low heat. The sugar melts and begins to brown. Stir constantly to prevent burning. Dilute this syrupy mass – it smells like a caramel candy – with water and dissolve by stirring. Depending on how intense you want the color to be, add caramel, stirring constantly, before bottling. Caramel, cooled and covered, can be stored for several weeks.

Dye plants

Safflower, curcuma (turmeric) and saffron are used to color foods, because of their strong dye effect.

Saffron is one of the most costly spices and also used as a coloring agent. 1 g saffron in 100 liters of mead gives an intense golden yellow color. It is best to add it during aging. Prior to bottling, carefully stir up the barrel contents, because the saffron settles to the bottom and the color will be concentrated there if you do not.

Vividly colored juices

Red juices especially are often used for coloring. These include currant, cherry, elderberry and red beet juice.

One liter of elderberry juice gives intense color to 100 liters of mead, without having any particular effect on the taste. You must use large amounts of cherry juice to get a good color, but this also means enhancing the mead's cherry flavor. Such honey wines are then served as "Odin's blood" or "Viking blood."

Besides making the corrections described above, you can also determine some important analytical values before bottling.

Key Analytical Values

It can be quite interesting for the individual mead brewer to know different analytical values for their mead. These values give information about:

- Longevity
- Balance or harmony
- Compliance with legal regulations

The most important parameters are the brewer's palate and nose. Sensory evaluation and analytical values help the wine maker decide whether and how the mead should be bottled.

What do the analytic values tell us before bottling, and what are they for?

- They help the brewer maintain consistent qualities over batches (residual sugar content)
- They determine the bottling process (hot or cold)
- They provide information if the mead still lacks sulfur or acidity

Which analytical values are useful?

- Alcohol content
- Residual sugar
- Sulfur content
- Acidity

Alcohol content

The countries listed below require a minimum alcohol content for mead, which must be met. The label must state the actual alcohol content.

Minimum alcohol content	
In **Germany**, minimum alcohol content is regulated by the "Guidelines for wine-like and sparkling wine-like beverages"	**5.5% ABV**
In **Switzerland**, minimum alcohol content is regulated by the "Regulation of the EDI [Swiss federal agency] for alcoholic beverages"	**7.0% ABV**
In the **USA**, minimum alcohol content is regulated by the "Revenue Act of 1918"	**7.0% ABV**

Apart from the legal framework, the level of alcohol content is an important indicator for selecting what bottling process to use. You can bottle a honey wine with 12.5 to 13% ABV and well-balanced residual sugar, using an almost-sterile bottling method. However, if the alcohol content is below 12.5% ABV, you risk possible re-fermentation in the bottle during prolonged aging, if you only do an almost-sterile bottling. Here, it is necessary to use either a hot or cold sterile bottling process.

The higher the honey wine's alcohol content, the lower the risk of re-fermentation in the bottle.

Residual sugar content

A honey wine's balance depends on such factors as the alcohol to residual sugar proportions.

> Mead with higher alcohol content can tolerate a higher residual sugar content without appearing sweet.

Such products are rich, powerful, and, due to its excellent qualities, can also be stored a long time.

It is interesting that honey wines with about 13% ABV are well received by most consumers. It is possible that this is because the ubiquitous "Coca Cola" and other sodas have similar residual sugar levels.

Sulfur content

Here again, the brewer must comply with legal regulations.

In Austria, total sulfur may not exceed 0.007 oz/qt (200 mg/l) and free sulfur just 0.0018oz/qt (50 mg/liter). The German regulations are similar.

The sulfur levels discussed in this book— 12 g/100 l when racking off the lees, and adding 12 g of wine sulfur before longer aging—will yield about 120 mg/l total sulfur in the wine. If you test again for free sulfur levels prior to bottling, this usually indicates an additional wine sulfur requirement of 10 g potassium pyrosulfite (KPS) per 100 liters. Thus, total sulfur content will be around 170 mg per liter. Testing results from a wine or must laboratory should serve to indicate if there is a basis for adding more wine sulfur.

Acidity

As already discussed in the chapter on "Mead starter solution" (page 26), acidity (in g/l or in titratable total acidity in parts per thousand) contributes both to the wine's taste balance and longevity. Here we find an optimum intersection point of these two qualities.

The goal is total acidity level of about 6 g per liter.

Analysis methods

Determining alcohol level

Malligand ebulliometer

The principle behind determining alcohol level using a Malligand ebulliometer, is to ascertain the wine's boiling point (pure alcohol has a boiling point of 172.94° F (78.3° C)) and infer the alcohol content from this. The first step is to measure the boiling point of water at the prevailing air pressure and adjust the device.

However, this method is not suitable for mead since it has a more or less heavy residual sugar content, which affects the boiling point—only fully fermented dry honey wines can be tested this way.

Distillation

This is a sure method to determine alcohol content and one wine laboratories like to use. Heat 100 ml of honey wine, which drives off (distills) the alcohol. The distilled alcohol is collected and topped off with distilled water, to 100 ml. You can then determine the alcohol level, using either an "oscillating density meter" or an alcohol spindle.

The advantage of this method is that it does not use any reagents, which must be constantly replaced.

Determining alcohol level with the Dr. Rebelein method

This method is the most sophisticated of those described here – both in equipment and number of reagents used. Using it only makes economic sense, if a large number of samples must be analyzed.

The beverage laboratory at the Warth Lower Austrian Beekeeping School

Determining acidity

The simplest method to determine acidity uses Bromothymol blue. The principle of measuring acidity with soda lye and Bromothymol blue is to keep adding lye of a known concentration to the mead sample until it reaches the neutral point, which will be shown by the color change. Then read the amount of lye used. This process is called "titration."

It determines the total titratable acidity. This refers to the sum of free acids in a beverage, with the exception of carbonic acid, which is removed from the sample before the test by heating and shaking.

Mead contains acids, which come either from the honey, fruit juice, or added acid.

Titratable acidity is expressed in g/l or parts per thousand.

In mead, average acidity levels are between 4 and 6 parts per thousand—therefore not nearly as high as in grape or fruit wines.

Equipment and chemicals

A 100 ml Erlenmeyer flask, 10 ml volumetric pipette, 10 ml graduated pipette or burette, fresh 2/15 n Bromothymol blue

Procedure

Measure 10 ml of mead into the Erlenmeyer flask using the volumetric pipette; then warm and shake it to remove the carbonic acid. After cooling to 68° F (20° C), use the graduated pipette or burette to add up to 2/15 n Bromothymol blue, until the transition point (from green to blue) is reached. Read the amount of Bromothymol blue used on the graduated pipette or burette; the value indicates g/l acidity, or parts per thousand.

Determining sugar level

Before fermentation, the best ways to measure sugar content are to use a refractometer (expensive) or a sugar spindle (cheaper); it measures in °Brix/°Oe. You cannot determine the residual sugar level in fermenting or fermented mead with a sugar spindle or refractometer, due to the development of alcohol, which changes the specific gravity and thus the density.

Since determining residual sugar in a fermented beverage is a more complex process, you should look for a specialized laboratory for this purpose.

The "Clinitest," which is readily and easily used for wine and fruit processing, has only limited use when brewing mead, because it can only determine residual sugar levels to 10 g/liter.

Residual sugar levels in fully fermented mead lie around 15 g/liter; in sweetened mead usually at 80 to 160 g/liter.

Analyzing lees stability

Honey contains substances which are ether poorly soluble and insoluble, such as waxes, dextrin, proteins, and pollen.

These substances can cause hard-to-eliminate sediment and filtration problems. Cloudiness caused by proteins is a special problem in already-bottled honey wines.

There are two ways to determine how stable the sediment is:

- Using a heat test
- "Bentotest"

Heat test

Keep a bottle of filtered mead at 104° F (40° C) for 12 hours, and then refrigerate it for 12 hours. If it doesn't become cloudy, you can consider the proteins in the beverage to be stable.

Dr. Jakob's "Bento test"

This test uses a reagent and its results can be evaluated in a short time. Filter a mead sample through a small filter until it is clear. then mix it with the reagent solution. If it becomes cloudy after a few minutes, this indicates the presence of proteins.

If the test shows proteins, then give the wine a series of preliminary finings using increasing amounts of bentonite.

The test using the smallest amount of bentonite, which yields negative results in a renewed "Bento test," gives the correct amount of bentonite needed for fining the wine.

Over-fining with bentonite will also affect the wine's color and taste.

Bottling

The goal is to bottle the mead so that it remains stable, with no other changes except those due to maturation, appropriate for its age.

Risk areas

There are two risk areas to watch for when bottling mead:

- Increased flocculation in the bottle due to unstable proteins
- Any start of re-fermentation in the bottle

Protein stability

Heat-sensitive proteins can flocculate in the bottle, due to temperature fluctuations or during the hot bottling, and cause persistent cloudiness.

In the chapter on "Clarification" (page 67), we gave an exact description of how to use the fining agent bentonite. In this chapter, we recommend that you use 200 g per 100 liters of mead, which should be sufficient, under normal circumstances, to bind any protein components, without weakening the mead's aromatic quality. It only makes sense to use larger quantities, if a wine or cider must laboratory made preliminary tests for the exact amount required; otherwise, the color and flavor of the honey wine will be affected.

There are two ways to test honey wine's stability in relation to thermolabile proteins:

1. Heat test

Keep a bottle of clear mead at 104° F (40° C) for 12 hours, and then refrigerate for 12 hours. Any heat-sensitive proteins will coagulate, making the wine cloudy or turbid.

This test is simple and significant.

2. Dr. Jakob's "Bento test"

The test is performed using a protein precipitation medium (reagent) and can be evaluated in a short time. Add a reagent solution to a mead sample. If it becomes cloudy after a few minutes, this indicates the protein contents.

If protein is detected, a series of fining processes using increasing amounts of bentonite is performed. The wine is filtered and again given a "Bentotest." The test that yields a negative "Bento test" result with the smallest amount of bentonite shows how much bentonite should be added to the barrel of mead. Over-fining with bentonite will remove all the proteins, but would also affect other qualities of the wine.

> Stability means the wine is microbiologically and chemically long-lived, which means it will not become cloudy or discolored, nor will it re-ferment in the bottle.

Re-fermentation in the bottle

This is certainly the greatest risk in marketing bottled honey wine. Re-fermentation will release more CO_2 and thus create more pressure in the bottle. It changes the smell and taste of the whole beverage. A light yeast sediment on the bottom is the least of the problems here.

> If CO_2 pressure becomes too great, the bottles can burst. Under product liability laws, the producer is legally responsible for all costs incurred.

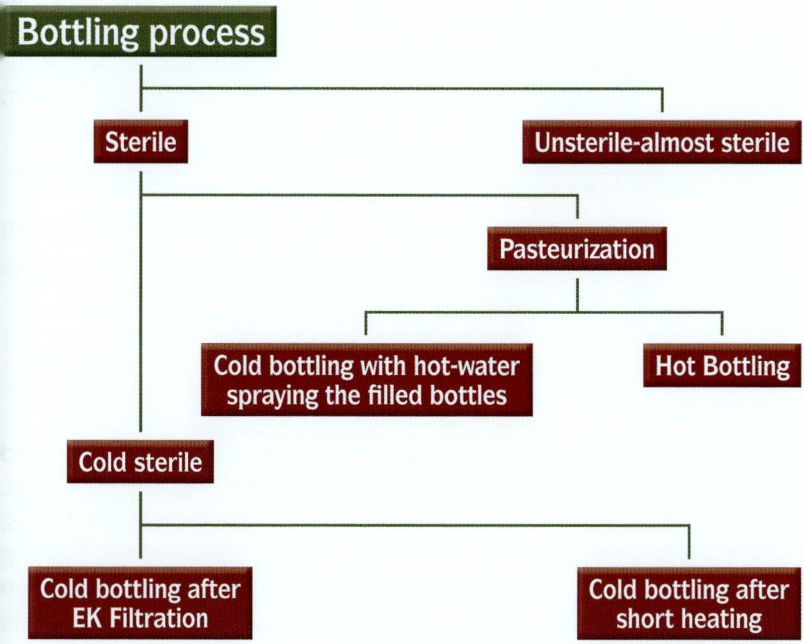

Re-fermentation is caused by the presence of sugar and yeast cells.

For mead brewers, this means:

- Either remove the yeast cells, or
- Inactivate them, or
- Try for an alcohol content in your honey wine high enough that the yeast can no longer multiply.

There are three ways to do this:

1. Hot bottling (inactivation of yeast)
2. Cold sterile bottling (removing the yeast)
3. Alcohol content of 13% ABV (internal stability)

Pasteurization

The principle of this bottling process is to kill the yeast cells by heating the beverage to 131° F (55° C.) To preserve fruit juices, 158° F (70° C) is required. However, since mead has an alcohol content of 10% ABV or more, pasteurization at 131° F (55° C) is sufficient. The combination of heat and alcohol inactivates the yeast.

Hot bottling

Heat the mead rapidly and fill the bottles quickly. Temperature is measured with a thermometer at the center of the bottle (bottle "core temperature"), which should be 131° F (55° C); the vessel is sealed and stood briefly on its head. This step ensures that the bottle neck and cap or cork are also wetted with the hot liquid, which kills any yeast cells present.

The simplest method is to heat in a saucepan on the stove or in a large kettle. Fill the bottles using a drain tap or a tube or hose.

Advantage: Simple method which doesn't require great effort
Disadvantages: It is hard to keep the temperature constant
Loss of aroma and alcohol

Baumann bell (sweet must bell)

Using a Baumann or sweet must bell both protects the product while increasing capacity. This process yields an hourly output of 60 to 200 liters.

A sweet must bell (Baumann bell) is a double-shell vessel. It is set in a water-filled pot, a water boiler, a steamer, or in an electrically heated boiler. The honey wine flows from an elevated container through the bell, which heats it. A thermometer in the outlet side and a regulating tap on the in-feed side, allow precise adjustments to the pasteurization temperature.

Advantages: Closed cycle system, meaning little loss of alcohol
High output per hour
Disadvantage: Technically more complex

Plate/Pipe heat exchanger

For processing larger amounts of wine, 150 l/hour and more, a plate or pipe heat exchanger functions better. These devices are available in various sizes and power levels. In plate Pasteurization, the beverage is fed through fine ducts. Using the counter-flow principle, hot water flows into an adjacent duct. The close contact of the two liquids in the ducts heats the mead. The quantity of mead being Pasteurized can be regulated by the flow rate and water temperature. Since this method of preservation requires a large amount of heat, you require a heavy boiler as the heat source. Portable, smaller devices, which can be gas-heated and are intended for multi-company use, are commercially available.

Line bottler with filter

Due to the high output per hour, all these devices require using a bottler, which is usually a four or six spigot line bottler.

Advantages: Closed cycle system with little loss of alcohol
High output per hour

Disadvantages: Technically complex
High investment costs

Electric Pasteurizer

This is a kind of pressure cooker with built-in flow-through coil. The mead flows through the built-in coil and is heated to Pasteurization temperature. A hot plate or an electric stove can be used as an additional heat source.

For all hot bottling methods:
Bottle core temperature between 131 and 176° F (55 and 60° C)
After sealing, the bottle is turned over for a short time
The filled bottles should be cooled as soon as possible after sealing
Corks are not suitable to cap the bottles, since the cork would be drawn into the bottle by the cooling and resulting vacuum
Champagne-style corks are also unsuitable because they do not seal tightly enough.
Screw caps, crown corks and swing stoppers are all suitable

Cold bottling with hot water spray

Fill the bottles with cold mead, then seal them and put in the Pasteurizer, where they are sprayed with hot water until the temperature in the bottle reaches about 131 to 140° F (55 to 60° C). The bottles are cooled again. The warming causes the contents of the sealed bottle to expand. To prevent bottles from breaking, leave about 3-4% free space during bottling.

There is a special chamber Pasteurizer for this purpose. Purchase and operating costs are relatively high.

Advantages: No loss of alcohol
High capacity
Precise temperature control
Disadvantages: Requires large space
High energy costs

There is a simpler solution for smaller amounts, which works on a similar principle:

Cold bottling while heating in a water bath

Place the cold-filled and sealed bottles in a water bath. Heat it until the bottle contents reach the desired Pasteurization temperature. Then drain the water off and slowly cool the bottles. A large cooking pot, a food processing dumper, as used in commercial kitchens, or a large copper kettle would all serve for the water bath.

Advantages: Easy way to make use of existing equipment
Less effort
Disadvantage: High energy costs

Cold sterile bottling

The purpose of this bottling method is to remove all harmful micro-organisms (yeasts, bacteria) which could cause re-fermentation or microbiological alteration through sterile filtration, and to fill and seal the bottles without any re-infection.

The most common bottling method used in wineries.

Due to the greater technical complexity, it only makes sense to use this bottling method if your enterprise makes, or intends to make, mead brewing into a business. In wine-growing regions, such bottling equipment is available for rent or for multi-enterprise ownership, but this would make it necessary to bottle larger quantities.

High-quality, small-sized equipment is suitable for this bottling processes in small businesses.

To do this, you must note and prepare the following:

- Sterile filters, pipes and bottler
- Sterile bottles
- Sterile caps
- Aseptic technique
- Keep machines and bottling area as clean as possible
- Prevent re-infection

To achieve these conditions, first thoroughly clean the entire bottling facility and then assemble and disinfect it.

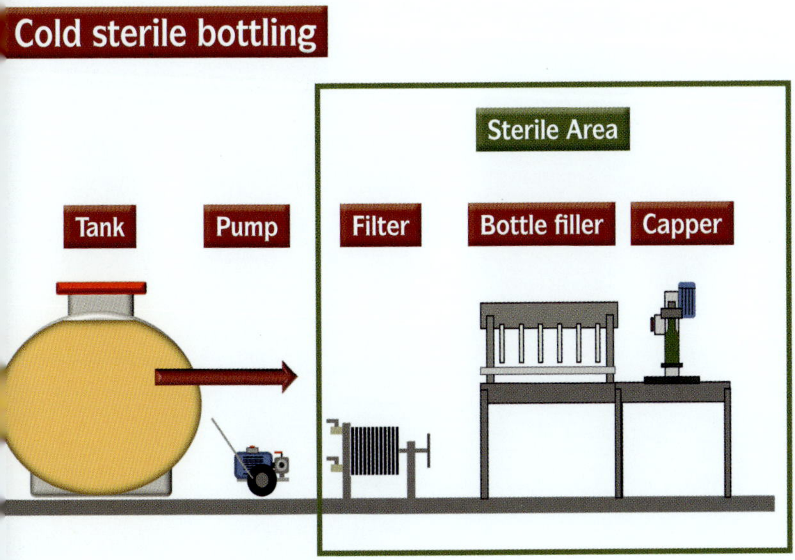

Left:
Bottling room with rotary bottle filler (top)
Rotary filler in operation (below)

Basic cleaning

There are specialized cellar cleansers available in specialty stores for basic cleaning, which either contain active chlorine compounds or are based on quaternary ammonium compounds (QUATS).

To ensure optimal cleaning, proceed as follows:

- The equipment should be taken apart as much as possible and put in the cleaning solution
- Remove all visible dirt using brushes and a water jet
- Thoroughly rinse off the cleaning solution with clean water

Critical areas to clean are seals, screw fittings, and the fine ducts of the filter.

Disinfection

Before the bottling day, fill the cleaned hoses, pump, the prepared filter and the bottler with a 3% hydrogen peroxide-based disinfectant, free from bubbles, and let stand for 12 hours. Attach bottles to the spigots on the filling machine, so that the spigots are also sterilized.

Before bottling, flush the disinfectant solution from the system with fresh water. Then, the honey wine will press the rinse water out of the filter, and bottling can begin.

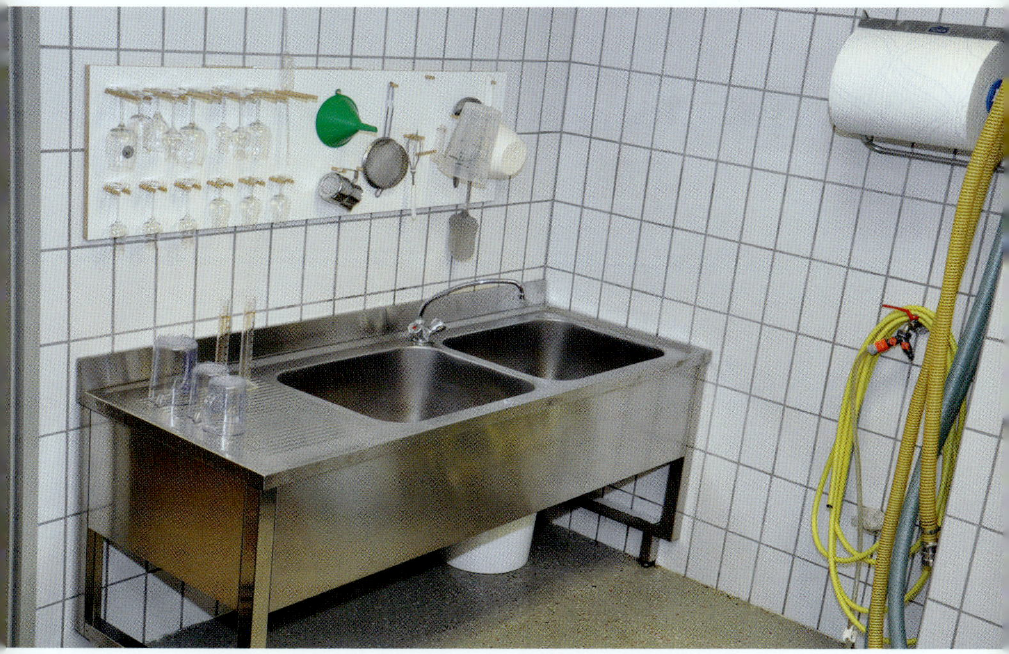

An optimally equipped hygienic area

The bottle sides must be absolutely clean, to prevent any infection. To do this, soak the dirty bottles in a special bottle cleaning solution a 104° F (40° C) for at least 20 minutes. Then get rid of any dirt with a bottle washing machine. Finally, rinse the bottles with fresh water and le them drip dry.

There are two ways to disinfect the bottles:

2% sulfurous acid	3% hydrogen peroxide solution
This method is hardly used today, because of the strong irritant effect	(such as Bisteril or P3 vino Oxi) spray for 2 seconds with the bottle sterilizer

For both options:
After sterilization, the bottles must be rinsed with water!

Bottle storage

Mead log

It might seem formal to recommend keeping a mead log or record. But whether you are just dealing with a carboy holding 26.4 qt (25 liters), or a fermentation tank with 528 qt (500 liters) or more – accurate records are essential for the following reasons:

- Even if you don't want to admit it, the truth is that after half a year, you will have a hard time remembering specific details such as temperature, volume and time intervals.
- Should faults occur in the mead, keeping accurate records will help you identify and avoid them in the future.
- A mead log lays the foundation for being able to brew more and more similar batches of mead.

"Who writes, stays with us."

You should keep such a mead log not just while preparing for fermentation, but until the final product is ready. This should also include simple sensory descriptions, with all the merits and—equally important—all the faults, to learn from them.

If you have accumulated experience from many mead logs over the years, it is interesting to browse through them and taste the honey wines they describe.

For your safety and that of your customers, you should keep exact records and samples of each batch of mead.

For an example of a mead record, see the next two pages.

Mead Log

Starting date: ____________________

Calculations:

Honey: Description:	kg:

Liters of starter:

Settings:	Degree Brix	Approx. % ABV	
	23.5	13	
	24.75	13.6	
	26	14.3	
	27	14.9	
	28.5	15.6	

	Amount/100 liter	In total amount
Lactic acid/citric acid		
Yeast nutrients:		
Pure culture yeast:		

Fermentation:
End of fermentation:

Test results after end of fermentation:

Alcohol content in % ABV.	Residual sugar in g/liter	Date

Racked off lees on:

Sweetening	kg of honey:	Variety	Date

	per 100 liters	In total amount	Date
Acidification			
Potassium metabisulfite			
Silica sol: Gelatin			
Bentonite: NaCalit XX			

Laboratory test results: free SO_2 in mg/liter:

Ideal: 25-40 mg/1 Calculated requirement: Amt. lacking x 2 = g/1000 liters

Added sulfur	Date	Amount in g/100 liter	In total amount

Filtration	Date	Type membrane

Preparation for bottling	Other treatments	Date

Bottling:	Filtration with	Number of layers	Date

Control data	Alcohol % ABV	Residual sugar g/l:	SO_2 Free	Total acidity

Batch number:	Number of bottles:	Bottling date:

Witham 1179 Friary
Friary Vintners Meads
TRADITIONAL MEAD
500 ml e
14% abv
another quality product from
Friary Vintners Limited
Witham Friary, Frome,
Somerset, BA11 5HD

Faults and diseases in mead

Mousiness

Sulfury

Lactic spoilage

Acetic acid

Woody taste

Oxidation

As with making grape and fruit wines, all common faults and diseases can occur in mead. Since we are dealing with a product which provides ideal conditions for the growth of microorganisms (bacteria, wild yeast) due to its high residual sugar content, the following are essential:

- Absolute cleanliness throughout the production process
- Continuous sensory testing of the product
- Work using very careful winemaking techniques
- Stabilize with free sulfur at 25-40 mg/liter

As we have stated, there are two main risk areas in mead brewing, which can lead to spoilage of the product:

1. Bacterial infection: This risk exists throughout the entire production process; the mead is most prone during fermentation.

2. Unstable wine in the bottle: start of re-fermentation, clouding and flocculation will spoil the honey wine.

Preventing bacterial infections

Steps taken	Results
Heating the honey before mixing with water/juice	Inactivates foreign yeasts
Rapid start of fermentation with yeast nutrients and adding a vigorously fermenting yeast	Basis for a clean fermentation
Fermentation temperature: 62.6 - 68° F (17-20° C).	Optimal fermentation conditions
Racking the wine off the yeast lees after fermentation ends, while adding 15 g KPS per 100 liters	Prevents yeast sulfur off-taste and bacterial diseases
Store tightly sealed	Eliminating oxygen in the barrel will deprive the microorganisms of an important requirement for life
Bottling: either "cold sterile" or "hot"	With both methods, we try to remove the yeast cells either mechanically or inactivate them using heat

These wine-making techniques are necessary to prevent growth of bacteria from the outset. Despite all precautions and wine-making techniques, the mead can become faulty. Below, we describe typical faults and diseases. These must be recognized at an early stage and treated quickly, to prevent complete spoilage.

Mousiness

Mousiness is one of the most feared "diseases" in mead brewing. Detecting it is relatively simple: the "aftertaste" is very unpleasantly bitter and above all, it persists for a very long time. Often, you only notice this bitter taste a few seconds after swallowing. Put a few drops of mousy mead on your palms, rub them and wait briefly; then you will notice unpleasant odor that is reminiscent of mouse urine – hence the name.

Causes

The primary cause is lactic acid bacteria, which can grow very easily in mead, because honey contains large amounts of gluconic acid. A delayed fermentation, caused by low acidity and high temperature, creates the ideal conditions for this disease.

Prevention

When brewing mead, it is essential to use faultless winemaking technique from the start; fermentation should begin rapidly; after fermentation stops, the lees must be racked off as quickly as possible, and wine sulfur added.

Cure

This disease is incurable. However, you can contain it, if, as soon as it occurs, you rack the mead immediately, aerate it well, and add wine sulfur. The term "aeration" means stirring up the wine in order to get as much air as possible into the beverage. You can do this using a spray nozzle, for example. The added oxygen dispenses the unpleasant flavors and odors. You should first try this method on a smaller amount of mead (1 liter), because the increased oxidation could also have the drawback of enhancing the growth of oxygen-loving microorganisms (acetic acid bacteria).

Mousiness is incurable.

Sulfur off-flavors

The smell of rotten eggs, garlic, cabbage, or onions most clearly describes the "sulfury" mead fault. On the palate, also, it has a broad and rotten taste.

You can verify if your honey wine is afflicted with hydrogen sulfide, by dropping a copper coin into a glass of the mead. After a short swish and rest in the mead, the copper will bind with the unpleasant rotten components in the wine.

Cause

This fault can come from sluggish fermentation, due to lack of nutrients, and/or by leaving the yeast in the honey wine for too long.

Prevention

The causes of hydrogen sulfide problems are very complex, and no mead make is protected against them. High fermentation temperature and fermentatior that is too intense increase likelihood that this fault will occur.

Therefore, as already stated frequently, ensure that you have:

- Sufficient yeast nutrients (N, P, vitamins)
- Fermentation temperature between 17-20° C
- Quick racking and clarification after fermentation ends

Treatment

When you find this fault, clarify the mead quickly with fining and filtration To a large extent, the off-odor clings to the sediment. Aerating the wine and adding wine sulfur can eliminate a minor hydrogen sulfide problem Another possibility is to use copper sulfate, but in this case, get the advice of a wine or must laboratory for this.

Lactic acid spoilage

The mead will have an unpleasant smell and taste like sauerkraut, usually soon after fermentation.

Cause

This group of bacteria multiplies very easily in low-acid products. Specific causes are limited fermentation, aerating too late, storing at temperatures that are too warm and failing to add wine sulfur.

Treatment

Racking off the lees – correcting acidity– adding wine sulfur with 15 g KPS per 100 liters – coarse filtering or fining, and ultimately, sterile filtration. Serious lactic acid spoilage cannot be cured. To prevent it, all vessels, filters and hoses must be disinfected.

Acetic acid

Both the nose and palate recognize a slightly sour, sharp, tone reminiscent of vinegar.

Causes

Acetic acid bacteria love air and warmth. Poor hygiene, failure to plug the container tightly after fermentation, failure to add wine sulfur, storing at high temperatures and insufficient fermentation can cause an acetic acid bacterial infection.

Prevention

Regular cleaning and disinfection are the most important measures, throughout the process. A rapid start to fermentation removes oxygen from the beverage. Don't use either the area or the equipment to make vinegar at the same time: there must be strict separation of area and equipment, or your mead can become contaminated by vinegar bacteria.

Cure

At the first signs, using a sterilizing filter will still work; in worse cases, the contamination is incurable. So as not to waste the product, you can make the mead into vinegar – as far away as possible from any place you will be brewing mead.

> Unsanitary winemaking will not only cause this bacterial disease; unsanitary work creates ideal conditions for many microorganisms to grow, including lactic and butyric acid bacteria, in addition to vinegar bacteria.

All the diseases caused by bacteria are almost impossible to cure. These diseases are infections which can be transmitted by blending and "sick" barrels, which can infect healthy honey wines.

Since a higher acid content is unpleasant, in mead the only preservatives are high alcohol content, absolute hygiene during winemaking, and sufficient protection by adding wine sulfur.

If these conditions are met, the living conditions for bacteria will be reduced enough to provide a very high degree of protection against these infections.

In addition to the typical bacterial diseases, mead can suffer other faults which will interfere with the flavor significantly.

These include:

- Woody taste from insufficiently seasoned oak barrels
- Faults due to overuse of either flavorings or citric acid
- Oxidation

Woody taste

A deliberately created woody taste is also known as "barrel aging."

If the mead brewer uses new wooden barrels, the alcohol in the honey wine will leach out the tannins contained in the wood. New barrels should be treated before the first filling, by leaching or steaming, to remove the existing tannins. This process is referred to as "seasoning." If the barrels are not seasoned, or are inadequately seasoned, the tannins dissolved in the mead will give it a flavor reminiscent of wood.

Blending with the other, fault-free mead can reduce this woody taste enough to eliminate any unpleasant character.

Oxidation

This easily preventable fault is a frequent problem, especially in mead brewing. A mead barrel which has not been plugged tightly enough, can stand for years in the cellar, without SO_2 protection. The mead will turn ever darker in color and becomes stale and flabby on the palate.

The basic principle is to introduce as little air as possible into the beverage, during the entire production process.

If tannic-rich fruit juices are added to the mead starter, oxygen can react with the existing polyphenols, causing a dark yellow to red coloration; this can also give rise to sediments.

Mead Recipes

Old mead recipes

To finish this book, I would like to present a collection of old – in part traditional – recipes. It may be that everyone will try these to see if they are suitable for brewing mead. A lot is certainly out of date, but we can still learn some things from these recipes.

It is interesting that, in almost every recipe, the mead starter is boiled before fermentation. This is the reason why mead had the image of a thick, syrupy, and very sweet drink. The high level of evaporation causes the entire liquid to thicken and the sugar to caramelize. The high sugar concentration makes the fermentation process correspondingly slow.

If you want to brew your mead according to one of these recipes, however, I absolutely recommend using a strong fermenting, pure culture yeast, to prevent spoilage during fermentation.

The well-known "father of beekeeping" Edmund Herold introduced the following recipe in his book *Heilwerte aus dem Bienenvolk* ("*Medicinal Qualities from the Bee Colony*"):

Hearty spiced mead

100 liters of water (tap or better rain water)
75 pounds of honey
10 grams each of tartaric and citric acid
5 whole cinnamon sticks
½ jar grated nutmeg
2 walnut-sized pieces of ginger
¼ packet ground cloves
"twice four fingers" of lemon balm tea.

Boil the honey solution for two hours, stirring constantly and skimming off the foam, so that the bad-tasting honey yeasts are killed and all the impurities removed. Add a half or whole stick of dissolved baker's yeast and add the spices in a small linen bag. Keep the room warm at 68-77° F (20-25° C). After about two months, when the vigorous as well as the weaker secondary fermentation is over, rack the wine for the first time. Bottle it after another six months.

Old mead recipe from East Prussia

To 1 quart (1 liter) honey, add almost 4 liters water
about 10 grams dried hops
1 sliced lemon and its peel
for brown coloring, add a few tablespoons of brown sugar

Bring all together to a boil, wrapping the hops and lemon slices in a bag so that it can be fished out easily. Stir well and fill one or more jugs up to ¾ full. Cover lightly because of the fermentation. Let stand at room temperature at least three weeks, until the mead is no longer fermenting. You can bottle the mead, not later than after one month.

As a precaution, don't cork too tightly.

Honey mead from the old master Dzierzon

Dissolve 5 liters honey in 20 liters of water and boil the solution until it holds up a fresh egg. The tip of the chicken egg should still show a bit above the liquid. Now, allow it to cool to roomtemperature, pour it into a wine barrel or carboy with a bung.

The rest is now a matter of taste; you can either leave the honey water as it is or, if you want the wine to be spicy, hang a little linen bag containing some nutmeg, cloves, ginger, and cinnamon in the liquid.

Let the liquid ferment for about six weeks, at moderate temperatures of 33.6 - 60.8 ° F (12-16° C). During fermentation, keep the barrel closed with a bung. When fermentation is complete, pour the mead into another, slightly smaller cask, but take care that no impurities from the sediment get into the fresh barrel.

Keep this barrel just lightly corked for the time being. After four to six months, all fermentation is over and the mead is ready for bottling, and can be racked into bottles. It then keeps for years and gains, from year to year, in aroma, flavor, and alcohol.

(From Guido Sklenar: *Imkerpraxis*)

Mead recipe from 1897

Pour 12 liters of water into a kettle, make a mark on the inner side of the kettle to show how high the water comes, and add 4 liters of water and 3.5 kilos of honey.

Boil and skim off the foam for half an hour, shake in a bare handful of very good hops (other recipes take two twigs of rosemary), and allow it to boil until the liquid has evaporated down to12 liters, as you can see from the mark you made on the side of the kettle.

Pour the brew into a wooden vat, let it cool briefly, mix in 4 tablespoons of fresh, good beer yeast, cover the vat with towels, tie them on and let it stand for 48 hours.

Then strain the liquid into a keg (carboy), hang in it a small linen bag containing 4 sliced lemons (no seeds), 4 tablespoons (30 grams) of crushed cinnamon, 3 tablespoons (15 grams) of cardamom, and 3 cloves. Close it with a bung and put it in the cellar for six to eight weeks. Then rack off the mead into bottles.

Mead Cocktails

Whether mixed with vodka, rum, honey liqueur, or other beverages, let your imagination run free. Add an impressive name like "stone thrower," "German turbo," or something similar and you have an exclusive drink for your next party!

Sparkling mead wine

To make a popular welcoming drink, mix champagne with mead 1:1. Depending on the character of the mead, the proportions can vary, but should be tested beforehand. Serve chilled in champagne glasses.

Mead punch I

Pour 2 bottles of mead over 1-2 cans mandarin oranges or pineapple and let it stand for 12 hours. Before serving mix in a bottle of champagne and 0.5 cup (100 ml) of blue orange liqueur (Curaçao).

Mead Punch II

Finely chop two large apples, drizzle some lemon juice over them and pour in 1.5 quarts (1.5 liters) of mead; let stand for one day. Before serving, add a bottle of sparkling wine. If the punch contains too much alcohol, you can dilute it with apple juice.

Viking blood

Mix mead 1:1 with cherry juice; drink it cold or warm.

Mulled mead with wine

Gently heat ½ liter of mead and mix in ½ tsp vanilla extract, about 8 cloves, ½ teaspoon ground cardamom, and 2 tablespoons rum. Let steep, strain out the cloves, and serve.

Mead cocktail

Mix 200 ml mead with 100 ml of orange juice. Add 50 ml of Danziger Goldwasser (spiced liqueur), and serve over ice cubes.

Hot mead with vodka –"Bowls you over"

To 1 l mead, add 7 cloves, 2 cinnamon sticks, ½ a grated nutmeg, ½ vanilla bean, and the juice of one lemon. Heat gently. After cooling, add 100 ml vodka and serve hot.

Melon punch with mead

Cut 1 small melon into small pieces, put in a punch bowl, pour over 1 liter mead and let stand for 12 hours. Before serving, add another quart 1 liter mead and ¾ liter sparkling wine. If you want a less alcoholic drink, replace 1 liter mead with 1 liter mineral water.

Mulled mead

Into (½ liter mead, mix carefully 1 teaspoon of vanilla sugar, 8 cloves, ½ teaspoon ground cardamom, and 2 tablespoons rum. Heat carefully (but don't let it boil) and allow it to steep. Strain out the cloves and serve warm.

Cooking with Mead

Wild boar with mead sauce

1 leg of wild boar (500 grams), boneless
Salt and pepper
3 sprigs thyme
200 milliliters strong meat stock
2 tablespoons crème fraîche
1 tablespoon honey
150 milliliters mead
Nutmeg
Salt and pepper
100 grams butter

Salt and pepper the wild boar leg and sear it on all sides. Put the meat in a roasting bag or cover with aluminum foil, adding 2-3 sprigs of thyme. Cook in the oven for 1 hour at about 195° F (90° C).

Add the stock to the pan drippings and cook down. Add 2 tbsp crème fraîche and 1 tbsp of honey to the liquid. Take it off the heat, and add the honey wine (mead). The high cooking temperature would change the taste of the honey wine; in the worst case, even make it bitter.

Season with grated nutmeg, salt and pepper. To bind the sauce, stir in the cold butter bit by bit. Before serving, add the juices from the meat to the sauce and stir in.

Viking blood jam

Mix ½ liter mead with ¼ liter cherry juice. Chop 250 g fresh sour cherries and add to the liquid. Mix with 500 g jelly sugar 2:1. Cook for 4 minutes. Make a "jelling test" and pour into jars.

Legal Regulations

Bibliography

Appendix

Legal regulations

We make no claim that our discussion of legal regulations in this chapter is complete. The relevant authorities will provide exact information on the currently applicable legal regulations!

The U.S.

U.S. Code–Title 27: Part 24: Wine; Subpart I–Production of Agricultural Wine

§ 24.200 General.

Agricultural wine may be produced on bonded wine premises from suitable agricultural products other than the juice of fruit. Water or sugar, or both, may be used within the limitations of this subpart in the production of agricultural wine. Agricultural wine may not be flavored or colored; however, hops may be used in the production of honey wine. Spirits may not be used in the production of the wine and a wine made from one agricultural product may not be blended with a wine made from another agricultural product. Agricultural wine made with sugar in excess of the limitations of this subpart is other than standard wine and will be segregated and clearly identified. Since grain, cereal, malt, or molasses are not suitable materials for the production of agricultural wine, these materials may not be received on bonded wine premises. Beverage alcohol products made with these materials are not classed as wine and may not be produced or stored on bonded wine premises.

§ 24.203 Honey wine.

(a Subject to paragraph (b) of this section, a winemaker, in the production of wine from honey, may add the following:

(1) Water to facilitate fermentation, provided the density of the honey and water mixture is not reduced below 13 degrees Brix;

(2) Hops in quantities not to exceed one pound for each 1,000 pounds of honey; and

(3) Pure, dry sugar or honey for sweetening. Sugar may be added only after fermentation is completed.

(b) After complete fermentation or complete fermentation and sweetening, the wine may not have an alcohol content of more than 14 percent by volume or a total solids content that exceeds 35 degrees Brix.

Switzerland

The Swiss Federal Department of Home Affairs (EDI), based on Article 4, paragraph 2, 26, paragraphs 2 and 5, and 27, paragraph 3 of the Food and Utility Articles of Nov. 23, 2005 (As of May 25, 2009)

Article and area of application – Art. 1

1. This regulation describes the following alcoholic beverages, determines the requirements and regulates their special identification and promotion/labeling:
   a. Wine, partially fermented grape must, new wine, partially fermented grape juice and wine-based drinks;
   b. Fruit and fruit wine, fermenting stone fruit juices, beverages of fruit or fruit wine and honey wine;
   c. Beer;
   d. Spirits;
   e. other alcoholic beverages.

6. Section: honey wine – Art. 38-Art. 39

Definition – Art. 38

Honey wine (mead) is a drink that is produced by alcoholic fermentation of a honey-water mixture.

Requirements – Article 39

1. Honey wine must have an alcohol content of at least 7 percent by volume.
2. The addition of sugars before the fermentation is prohibited.
3. Flavoring with spices and herbs is allowed.

Identification – Art. 3

1. For alcoholic beverages with an alcohol content of more than 1.2 percent of volume, the alcohol content must be specified in "% vol." The actual content may vary from the declared content, both above and below, at most by 0.5 percent by volume.
2. For sweet alcoholic beverages of any composition, which might be confused organoleptically with non-alcoholic soft drinks such as sodas, table drinks, nectars, fruit juices and iced tea (e.g. "alcopops"), the following instructions apply:
   a. "alcoholic soft drink," and
   b. "Contains x % alcohol by volume."

   The information referred to in paragraph 2 must appear in the same place as the product description.

Austria

Codex chapter B3 – Sub-chapter mead honey wine

Description

1. As mead (honey wine), is understood for the purposes of this sub-chapter, a drink made from a honey solution (a mixture of honey as defined in honey regulations and drinking water in terms of drinking water regulations, of at least one part honey to two parts water) which is produced by fermentation.

   It has, originating from the honey used, typical smell and flavor characteristics. Spices, herbs, fruits and fruit juices can be added in small amounts only for flavor enhancement.

   Wine with added honey (in the sense of the Wine Act 1999, as amended) is not covered in this sub-chapter.

2. The alcohol content of the mead is at least 11 % volume and may only be introduced by means of fermentation.

3. To support fermentation and clarification, for wine-making practices and processes (within the meaning of Wein G 1999, as amended), it is allowed to use standard technological aids (i.e., pure culture yeasts, yeast nutrients, clarifiers) for the production of mead.

4. Mead (honey wine) is clear: it is usually filtered before bottling.

5. According to the regulations on other additives such as colorants and sweeteners BGBl. [Federal Law Gazette] II 383/1998, as amended, the preservatives sorbic acid and sulfur dioxide can be added to mead. The maximum amounts for each are 200 mg/l.

6. Mead (honey wine) can also be preserved by heat treatment during bottling.

7. The addition of acidifiers such as citric acid is common and governed by the provisions of the regulations on other food additives such as colorants and sweeteners, BGBl. II 383/1998, as amended.

8. Flavorings, according to the flavor regulations, BGBl. II 42/98, as amended, are not to be added. Adjustment of the taste after fermentation with honey is possible.

9. There are also mixtures of mead (honey wine) with different-flavored foodstuffs on the market, in which the characteristic odor and taste properties of pure mead (honey wine) are no longer prominent, or are overlaid. Such products are not regulated by this Codex sub-chapter and are to be identified accordingly.

Identification of mead (honey wine)

10. Products manufactured according to these guidelines, are identified as "mead," also in conjunction with the words "honey wine." These can be referred to by the (traditional) Austrian Codex quality.

11. The allowable deviation, for the information on alcohol content according to § 4, line 9 of the Food Labeling Regulation, BGBl. 72/1993, as amended, for mead (honey wine) is, under alcohol information regulations, BGBl. II No. 136/1997) ± 1 vol -%.

12. Notations such as "dry," "semi-sweet," "sweet" or similar, refer to the average overall impression and are provided only as a guidance for consumers.

Germany

The legal bases for the production of honey wine, sparkling honey wine and honey wine with fruit juice or fruit wine, form the: "Guidelines for wine-similar and sparkling wine-similar beverages," in the version of 27 November 2002, most recently amended on 06/16/2008.

1. Definition:

Honey wine is an alcoholic beverage, made from a weight of honey and max. two parts by weight of water (drinking water quality), using partial or complete alcoholic fermentation; with no addition of types of sugar or sweetening ingredients.

2. Permitted production processes:

- Technical procedures (extraction)
- Filtration
- Centrifugation
- Thermal treatment
- Air and oxygen treatment
- Treatment processes (extraction)
- Addition of liquid pure yeast or dry yeast
- Addition of yeast nutrients: max. 40 g/100 l of ammonium salts
- Addition of max. 3 g/l citric acid
- Potassium pyrsulfite or metabisulfite up to 200 mg/l in the finished product calculated as SO2
- Caramel for color correction
- Sorbic acid or potassium sorbate up to 200 mg/l in the finished product
- Clarifying agents such as gelatin, silica sol, bentonite
- Hops, spices

3. Quality characteristics:

- at least 5.5-% ABV existing alcohol
- at least 16 g/l sugar-free extract, without added acid
- at most 1.2 g/l volatile acid, calculated as acetic acid

4. If no additives are used, ...

... this should be indicated on the label: i.e., "no added preservatives" "without the addition of acidifiers"

5. Name, label information:

- "Honey wine" or "mead" or both
- Name, address of the producer or bottler
- Actual alcoholic strength in % vol. (Tolerance limit + 0.5% vol.)
- Lot number or bottle filling number
- Nominal filling amount

Bibliography

Maier-Bruck, Franz: Vom Essen auf dem Lande (From Eating in the Countryside), (Kremayer & Scheriau, Vienna 1981).

Herold, Edmund: Heilwerte aus dem Bienenvolk (Medicinal Qualities from the BeesColony), (Ehrenwirth, 9. Edition, Munich 1984).

Zander/Maurizio: Der Honig (Honey), (Eugen Ulmer, Stuttgart 1975).

Stückler, Karl: Most und Apfelwein, (Cider and Apple Wine), (Leopold Stocker, Graz 2009).

Schandler/Koch/Kolb: Fruchtweine (Fruit Wines), (Eugen Ulmer, Stuttgart . Edition 1981).

Horn/Cord: Das große Honigbuch (The Large Book of Honey) (Ehrenwirth, Munich 1992).

Dittrich, Helmut H.: Mikrobiologie des Weines (Microbiology of Wine), (Eugen Ulmer, Stuttgart 1987).

Conversion Tables

With few exceptions such as ABV, exactness of measurement is not a requirement for making mead. This chart offers metric measures, with English equivalencies in more common terms as well as more accurate approximations. Conversion programs abound on the internet.

WEIGHT

Metric	U.S. Units *ACCURATE*	U.S./U.K. Common *(EST.)*
1 mg	.015 grains	–
2 mg	.031 grains	–
5 mg	.077 grains	–
10 mg	.154 grains	–
20 mg	.308 grains	–
30 mg	.462 grains	–
40 mg	.617 grains	–
50 mg	.771 grains	–
60 mg	.926 grains	–
70 mg	1.08 grains	–
80 mg	1.23 grains	–
90 mg	1.39 grains	–
100 mg	1.54 grains	–
1 g	0.04 oz	–
2 g	0.07 oz	–
3 g	0.10 oz	–
4 g	0.14 oz	–
5 g	0.18 oz	–
6 g	0.21 oz	–
7 g	0.25 oz	–
8 g	0.28 oz	–
9 g	0.32 oz	–
10 g	0.35 oz	–
20 g	0.70 oz	–
30 g	1.05 oz	–
40 g	1.40 oz	–
50 g	1.75 oz	–
100 g	3.5 oz	–
200 g	7.0 oz	–
500 g	17.5 oz	–
750 g	26.25 oz	–
1 kg	35 oz/2.2 lb	–
2 kg	4.4 lb	–
3 kg	6.6 lb	–
4 kg	8.8 lb	–
5 kg	11.0 lb	–
10 kg	22.0 lb	–
50 kg	110.3 lb	–
75 kg	165.3 lb	–
100 kg	220.5 lb	–

VOLUME

Metric	U.S. Units *ACCURATE*	U.S./U.K. Common *(EST.)*
50 ml	1.7 oz	10 teaspoons
100 ml	3.4 oz	7 tablespoons
125 ml	4.2 oz	7 tablespoons
250 ml	8.5 oz	0.5 cup
500 ml	17 oz	1 pint
1 liter	33.8 oz	1 quart
2 liters	67.7 oz	2 quarts
3 liters	101.4 oz	3 quarts
4 liters	135.5 oz	4 quarts/1 gallon
5 liters	169.1 oz	5 quarts
6 liters	202.9 oz	6 quarts
7 liters	236.7 oz	7 quarts
8 liters	270.5 oz	8 quarts/2 gallons
9 liters	304.3 oz	9 quarts
10 liters	338.1 oz	10 quarts
15 liters	507.2 oz	15 quarts
20 liters	676.3 oz	20 quarts/5 gallons
30 liters	1014 oz	30 quarts
40 liters	1353 oz	40 quarts/10 gallons
50 liters	1691 oz	50 quarts
50 liters	1691 oz	50 quarts
75 liters	2536 oz	75 quarts
100 liters	3381 oz	100 quarts
150 liters	5072 oz	150 quarts
200 liters	6763 oz	200 quarts/50 gallons